Coaching Youth Soccer

Coaching
Youth Soccer

The European Model

Kevin McShane

McFarland & Company, Inc., Publishers
Jefferson, North Carolina, and London

Library of Congress Cataloguing-in-Publication Data

McShane, Kevin, 1966–
    Coaching youth soccer : the European model / Kevin McShane.
        p.   cm.
    Includes bibliographical references (p.) and index.
    ISBN 0-7864-1088-4 (softcover : 50# alkaline paper) ∞
    1. Soccer for children — Coaching — Europe.   2. Soccer for
children — Coaching — United States.   I. Title.
GV943.8.M38   2002
796.334'07'7 — dc21   2001031556

British Library cataloguing data are available

Manufactured in the United States of America

Cover photograph ©2001 Index Stock

*McFarland & Company, Inc., Publishers
    Box 611, Jefferson, North Carolina 28640
    www.mcfarlandpub.com*

For Kelly —
who makes all my dreams come true.

Acknowledgments

As coaches always should, I want to thank the many people who helped make this effort possible. As coaches also must do, I want to say that the strengths of this book are due to the assistance of these people and that I take responsibility for any mistakes or weaknesses.

I must begin with thanks to my family. My wife, Kelly, encouraged me to take a sabbatical in Europe so that I could do the research for this book. She also hounded me to make sure I actually did the writing and then was kind enough to edit my initial drafts. My children, Molly (who is right-footed) and Michael (a lefty), are a constant source of soccer and other kinds of fun.

My father, Clay McShane, and my friend, Rick Lawes, read drafts of the book and provided many useful ideas.

I also want to thank my other family, the one at St. Albans School. I look forward to work every day. I would especially like to thank the boys in the Total Soccer Program, who have provided me with many great moments over the years.

Major thanks to Graham Ramsey. He has provided many other coaches and me with stimulating ideas about the game of soccer, as well as exposed us to the styles of great coaches from all over the world. It was he who opened the door for my European odyssey.

Rudolf Psotta, the head instructor of the Czech "A" license course and my friend, provided answers to many of my questions about the game in the Czech Republic. One of my fondest memories of the year in Prague was being invited to share the traditional Czech Christmas carp with him and his family. My other professor, Mario Buzek, is one of the most insightful soccer people I have ever met.

I thank the people at the clubs I visited: Ludek Prochazka at Slavia Prague, Ludek Klusacek at Bohemians Prague, Llorenc Serra Ferrer at

Barcelona, Ernst Tanner at Munich 1860, Willie McStay at Glasgow Celtic, and Alan Irvine at Newcastle United. Their hospitality and generosity were first class.

The boys from Dynamo Zizkov ("world's greatest expat football team") have my gratitude for helping to keep me sane during my year in Prague. I am indebted to my teammate Nick Carey who translated an article about Bayern Munich's youth program from Czech to English.

Also in the mental-health-while-in-Prague department, I would like to thank the Sasser and Dode families, whose friendship I cherish.

Finally, I have been lucky to know many great coaches since I started my involvement with organized sports: Richard Quigley, Leo Lanzillo, Jape Shattuck, Guy Fraiture, Keith Tabatznik, Graham Ramsey, David Baad, Doug Boswell, and Skip Grant among them.

I want to thank specially my first and still my best-ever coach, my dad.

Tenleytown
Summer, 2001

Table of Contents

Preface

It is sometimes difficult for me to sit at matches with soccer coaches and coaching instructors who are so busy being erudite and analytical about the game of soccer that it seems beneath them to show any emotion about what happens on the field. To me, the emotions are what make sports, and especially soccer, great. The joy and agony that soccer provides for the players, coaches, and spectators are the best part of the game. The first things I think of in soccer are the great (and the terrible) moments.

The chapter entitled "The Greatest Moment Ever" in *Fever Pitch* by Nick Hornby sums it up better than I ever could. In that chapter he vividly describes the culmination of his 18-year wait for his beloved Arsenal to win the English championship, a victory which happens on a last-second goal in the last game of the season. The feeling of pure joy he shares still gives me goosebumps every time I read it. Of course, we all have our own favorite moments.

Some of my favorite moments include celebrating after we won a tournament as kids, seeing grown men weep in the Rose Bowl as Brazil lifted the World Cup in 1994, witnessing David O'Leary making his penalty to put Ireland through to the World Cup quarterfinals in 1990, seeing Eddie Pope score the winner in the first Major League Soccer final, being stunned as Michael Owen scored for England against Argentina in the 1998 World Cup, and winning the school's first league championship in 17 years with the high school team I coach.

This book is ostensibly about the development of youth soccer players. I hope that ultimately it is also about how we can all share more of the magic moments by developing better players. Millions of people all over the world love to watch soccer matches. From watching them myself, the question that always has nagged at me is: "How did the players get there?" How did these players prepare to be world class professionals? I hope this

1

book goes some way towards explaining how the current players got where they are and how we can help more people, especially more Americans, get there in the future. As the United States' last place showing at the World Cup in 1998 showed, we have a lot of work to do.

This book is for coaches, managers, and administrators of youth soccer, primarily in the United States, but also for people involved with youth soccer all over the world. I hope that within its pages, readers will find insight into how some of the top clubs in Europe run their youth player development programs. Youth soccer leaders will be able to use the comparisons among the clubs and the youth training in their own countries to see what they might do to improve youth soccer and the preparation of elite players.

When observing how a soccer club operates, two things are particularly worth noting. The obvious one is how the clubs develop their youths as soccer players. The second but more important one is how the clubs keep perspective and balance to make sure the young people have fun and develop as human beings.

No person, team, or country should try to imitate a model to the point that it tries to become something it is not. However, we can all learn from different sources and incorporate what will work for us. From the information I have found, I will make suggestions about how we might improve youth soccer in the United States. Maybe, the changes will some day bring the U.S. team closer to first place at the World Cup — but more importantly, the changes may help us keep better perspective on what is really important in youth soccer: *fun and learning.*

This book concentrates on male soccer, for two reasons: First, there is so little soccer for females outside the United States (and a few other countries) that it is difficult to study it abroad. Indeed, many other countries would do well to study the opportunities available to female players in the United States. Most countries are well behind the U.S. in terms of access to the game for girls and women. Second, the United States is currently the women's world champion, so we must be doing something right.

Research Process

I researched this book during the 1999-2000 soccer season in Europe. The school where I teach and coach, St. Albans in Washington, D.C., granted me a leave of absence to live in Prague, Czech Republic, for one year. While in Prague I studied for the Czech Football Federation (CMFS) "A" License, also known as the Union of European Football Associations

(UEFA) A Level License. I also watched a lot of professional matches, observed youth leagues, and coached.

In terms of professional matches, there are four teams of the Czech first division in Prague. Most weekends, therefore, I could attend two top-level professional matches. I also watched as Sparta Prague competed in the two group stages of the European Champions League and as Slavia Prague made a run to the quarterfinals of the UEFA Cup. I visited matches from the 3rd, 4th, and even 5th divisions of Czech soccer leagues as well as some games of the Czech national team (there were no second division teams in Prague). Additionally, I went on a regular basis to watch the training of the professional team of Sparta, as well as the youth teams of Sparta and Slavia.

Another way I spent my time was observing youth leagues. The Czech Republic has national under 18 and under 16 leagues, from which I saw many matches. I also went to matches for local youth leagues. I concentrated on Slavia's youth system because they have a large complex so that all of their youth teams train in one place, which made observation easier. Finally, while in Prague, I coached the fourth grade team at the international school my daughter attended and ran a soccer group for my three-year-old son and his friends.

I also spent significant time outside of Prague, with one-week stays at some clubs in other European countries. These clubs included FC Barcelona, TSV Munich 1860, Glasgow Celtic FC, and Newcastle United FC. On each of these trips (as well as a few family trips), I viewed some professional matches and searched for books and magazines which contained information on coaching and youth development schemes. The most interesting book I found was a compilation of interviews with legendary Dutch player and coach Johan Cruyff from throughout his career as a player and coach. Cruyff's comments in *Ajax, Barcelona, Cruyff: The ABC of an Obstinate Maestro* were fascinating. I have quoted him frequently in this book. At best his comments are brilliant; at worst they are at least thought-provoking.

All of this activity was supplemented by the games I watched on television, of which there were a *few* (although no more than are available with a satellite dish in the United States and *certainly* no more than my wife would tolerate!).

I have attempted to include information from all of these sources in the book. The books and magazines which I have cited or consulted are listed and described briefly in the Annotated Bibliography.

Outline of the Book

Chapter 1, "The State of American Youth Soccer," is an overview of youth soccer in America today, with an emphasis on programs for elite players. It is based primarily on my own 25 years of experience in the game. I believe it highlights the need for study of how other countries develop their players.

The next five chapters review different aspects of the European clubs. In each chapter, I will highlight two clubs as case studies. While every club had some unique aspects, there was a great deal of similarity among them. I will also provide unique or interesting ideas from the other clubs that I visited and my search of soccer literature in each chapter.

These several chapters break down in the following manner. Chapter 2, "Organization, Facilities, and Equipment," reviews the nuts and bolts of the youth development departments at the soccer clubs. The organization, facilities, and equipment are interesting because they provide context for the youth training and they offer a chance to compare clubs to one another and to what occurs in the United States.

Chapter 3, "Player Evaluation," focuses on how clubs find players. The first activity of a youth development scheme is to have players to develop, and this chapter looks at how they are selected, evaluated, and retained. This chapter also reviews what happens to players who are released.

Chapter 4, "Training Timetable and Components," analyzes training methods and match play in the clubs that I visited (although specific training exercises are not taken up until the appendices). How often do the players train and what components are there in the training? It includes the areas of soccer-specific training, as well as psychological development, physical training (coordination and conditioning), nutrition education, and how clubs look after players' academic (or vocational) work. While the training timetables do indicate how much goalkeeper training the clubs have, the chapter (and the exercises in Appendix B) includes very little information about the training of goalkeepers. My focus was on field players. Chapter 4 is essential reading for coaches designing training programs for their teams. It highlights the ways in which European players spend a lot more time training, and how that training develops them holistically.

Chapter 5, "Coaching," considers the coaches in these clubs. There are five key areas for coaches: knowledge (including their training and credentials), experience, ongoing education, ability to teach and pass on what they know to their players, and commitment to their players.

Chapter 6, "Philosophy of Youth Soccer in Europe," reviews the philosophies of the different clubs' youth training programs. It looks at questions such as why they run youth programs and what their goals are, how a club's activities and atmosphere compare with its stated philosophy, and how clubs handle difficult issues in youth development. There is a sense of perspective in the goals of the European youth soccer programs, a perspective too often absent in youth soccer in the United States.

Chapter 7, "Recommendations for the United States from European Clubs," contains conclusions and recommendations on what youth coaches and others in the United States can learn from the European experience, and how they can use it to strengthen the youth soccer system in the country.

The appendices include the questionnaire and samples of training exercises from the various clubs. The reason that I included training exercises only in the appendices is that I do not believe that they are the problem with American youth soccer. There is no "magic drill," or set of drills, which will automatically produce world class players. Training exercises are only a vehicle which a coach can use to help stress a point or to teach techniques through repetition. As I will make clear, one of the main points of this book is that it is not so much what exercises players do at practice, but rather how coaches interact with players within drills, games, and training exercises that makes the difference.

The bibliography lists many excellent articles and books on soccer. I recommend all of them for reading independently.

Notes About Word Choices

Throughout the book, I have used American terms such as "soccer" and "field" (rather than "football" and "pitch"). When quoting European speakers and writers I have substituted these terms. On the other hand, I have used the European word "physiotherapist" in place of what Americans usually call a "trainer," the person who tapes ankles and goes on the field to assist injured players. Some clubs also have physiologists, scientists who study and advise coaches and players about neuromuscular activity during exercise. Physiologists' work includes reviewing the energy input and output of an athlete and the technique of movement in an activity.

By using the words above in the ways I have described, I have attempted to make the text clearer.

Because my research involved male players and coaches, I have used "he" throughout the book. In most places, it is possible to read as "he or she."

A Final Note

It is my opinion that, considering the population and wealth of the United States and the number of American youth who participate in soccer, the country should be able to produce players who can compete successfully at the highest levels of the game. My hope is that this book will help us improve the ways we work with children so that they will be better players and better people when they reach adulthood.

Chapter 1

The State of American Youth Soccer

From the perspective of player development, we must embrace the viewpoint that growth is a process. Players do not develop in just one season; it takes several years. Unfortunately, many young players are either selected out, or drop out at too early an age, largely because playing is no longer enjoyable. Players need to play fast, think fast, and act fast, but in order to develop these fast players, we need to maintain their interest in the game. Speed is relative. In our fast pace society, in order to develop the brilliant player, we need to slow down in order to go further.

— Dr. Ronald Quinn,
Head Women's Soccer Coach, Xavier University[1]

Youth soccer is booming in the United States. The numbers of children playing soccer compare well with other, more traditional, American sports such as basketball, baseball, and American football. If you drive around an American city on a weekend, you cannot avoid seeing kids playing soccer. Indeed, if you stumble across one of the growing number of "soccer parks," you are likely to see hundreds of kids playing at the same time. For those who love soccer, it is an exciting prospect that so many youth players might translate into success internationally. It certainly has already on the female side. In 1999, the United States Women's Team won the World Cup. Even if all of the youths playing soccer do not translate into the U.S. men's team lifting the World Cup, it is worth studying the activity of so many children.

Given the game's popularity with children, it is disappointing to me that many players stop playing or having any involvement in the game when they reach secondary school and teams become more selective. In

7

short, most young players do not remain interested in the game. On the elite level, as shown by the U.S. team's disappointing performance at World Cup 1998 in France, the U.S. is not turning out the number of solid international class players that the youth numbers indicate the country should. Countries with a fraction of the United States' population and registered players develop more top-class players and teams. For example, nations such as the Czech Republic and Nigeria have not only fewer players but also fewer resources in terms of facilities, equipment, and coaches. However, their teams do well internationally. Perhaps our players are missing out on something in their development.

To me there are important questions of pedagogy here. What are youth players in the United States currently learning in our youth system? What activities do the youth players in European clubs undertake? How can we improve our system so our youth players can learn more?

As we will see, the European clubs believe that there is more to being a professional than just soccer training. Top soccer players are more than just people who can juggle the ball a lot. Top-class players are those capable of competing in the best leagues in the world (Italy, England, Germany, and Spain, for examples). American players who can play in these leagues will also make the United States men's national team competitive in the World Cup.

While we should be interested in retaining people in the game in every capacity (players, coaches, administrators, referees, and spectators), the main focus of this book is developing better players. We will study how European clubs develop their players to see if there are any lessons to be learned from them for developing players in the United States.

A survey of soccer literature, particularly coaching books and internet sites, reveals the right messages. Coaching books generally include a lot of training exercises for coaches to use. Since coaches *should* always be looking for new ideas and new ways to train, that is good. (It is also the reason I have included a number of training exercises from my research in Europe in the appendices of this book.) More importantly, coaching books often include sections on the philosophy of youth soccer: how the focus should be on having fun and learning. There are many soccer programs in the United States that keep these goals in mind through finding proper coaches and through league rules. For example, the American Youth Soccer Organization (AYSO) has rules and codes of conduct for all people involved, to make sure that they keep proper perspective on what they are doing. The AYSO does well, in personal development terms, because it respects that youth sports should be a fun activity in which there is value in simply playing. The AYSO's playing focus is strictly recreational.

It is a paradox of developing youth soccer players that while fun and learning must be part of the experience, if we are to develop top players the level of play must be intense. When the intensity is increased, it becomes difficult to keep perspective on personal development, fun, and growth as a player. For example, a high level of play implies selection, both by players who are interested and coaches who must choose players. It also involves more competitive play than recreational soccer, since players will only improve when presented with challenges. My experience has been that at the elite levels, where top players must develop, those involved in youth soccer in the U.S. are not able to balance personal development with technical development as a player, but rather are carried away by very different priorities.

The remainder of this chapter is divided into four parts:

- A description of the current youth soccer scene in the United States, primarily using anecdotes from my own experience. By looking at various aspects of youth soccer, one can gain a sense of where American youth soccer stands. The subsections, "Organization, Facilities, and Equipment," "Player Identification," "Training Timetables and Components," "Coaching," and "Philosophy," give information on the state of American youth soccer. There is also a brief summary at the end of the section. The topics of each of the subsections are the topics of later chapters in which I will review European youth soccer programs.
- An analysis of whether the United States' youth soccer system is producing top-class soccer players.
- Observations about what kind of people I believe this system sends out into society.
- A conclusion containing remarks summarizing the state of American youth soccer.

Youth Soccer Today in the United States

The United States finished fourth at the Under 17 World Cup in 1999, seemingly placing the United States in the elite of world soccer. The three teams ahead of the United States were Brazil, Australia, and Ghana. Most people in soccer consider Brazil one of the top, if not the top, soccer nation in the world. However, Ghana has never played in the full World Cup, and Australia has only played in one. It appears, therefore, that the correlation between success at Under 17 level and senior level is very low. How did the United States achieve such a result in 1999, and will that success translate into success for the senior national team? To find out, we must analyze what is occurring in American youth soccer.

During my stay in Europe, I found that European coaches are curious about youth soccer in the United States. They have heard about the large participation numbers and they want to know how it works. I had difficulty answering them. America is so big and the people are so diverse that there are many answers to every question.

Soccer was kept alive in the United States until the 1970s by ethnic leagues, private schools, and colleges. Over time, many ethnic teams and leagues lost their popularity as second- and third-generation Americans did not want to play their fathers' game from the "old country." They turned to more "traditional" American sports such as American football and baseball. Thankfully, the schools and the North American Soccer League (the NASL and its predecessors) not only kept the game alive, but also helped it grow in the suburbs of American cities. These factors have contributed to the current state of American soccer.

In 1995, 2.9 million children ages 6 to 18 were registered with the three youth soccer groups in the United States: United States Soccer Federation (USSF), AYSO, and the Soccer Association for Youth (SAY). Just 10 years earlier, there were 1.5 million registered players. There are also many more youth players who play in unaffiliated youth leagues. In secondary schools, there were 464,000 soccer players in 1995, almost double the 256,000 of 10 years before.[2] It is important to remember that approximately 40 percent of the participants are female.

The game is played in all 50 states and the District of Columbia. Youth soccer ranks among the most popular sports activities for American children. Approximately 20,000 spectators visit the collegiate national championships on the men's side and roughly 7,000 spectators view the women's final. The men's collegiate championship actually turns a small profit through gate receipts, one of the very few collegiate championships to do so.

The lack of history in soccer was a positive factor in its early growth. The growth started in the 1970s during the boom years of the NASL. At many youth programs' inception, the goal was simply participation. Many of the people involved in starting youth soccer programs did not see other youth sports and their professional equivalents creating a proper developmental environment for their children. With a new sport, there were no negative role models and no parents making it too competitive. In the words of one coach, who helped start the youth soccer program in my hometown of Arlington, Massachusetts:

We wanted to make sure that everyone got a chance to play: including girls, the athletically challenged, and back-up players on select teams. Little leagues (baseball) and kindred groups sat too many kids on the bench or cut them. We also wanted the kids doing something with a higher fitness value and less direct control during a game than the traditional American sports. I think that we succeeded in all those goals. This attitude can't turn out elite teams and, in fact, leaves elite teams to people who are often quite crazy.

While "recreational" teams provide many advantages to the kids who play on them, they cannot provide the high-level play that elite teams do. As the game has grown and players in the United States have tried to maximize their ability in the game, the need has arisen to manage the growth of the game.

ORGANIZATION, FACILITIES, AND EQUIPMENT

Most European countries have a single governing body for soccer and a single system of player development. In the United States, there are many governing bodies and many paths a player can choose (or have chosen for him) in his development. For example, there are different national organizations such as the United States Youth Soccer Association (USYSA), SAY, and AYSO. Beyond that, there are local leagues run by Boys and Girls Clubs, YMCAs, CYOs, and other groups.

As this book is about developing top-class players, I will focus on USYSA. In addition to playing on USYSA affiliated teams, elite American youth players are also involved in soccer at their schools and at soccer camps. A branch of the USSF, USYSA is affiliated with elite youth teams. The USYSA sponsors youth national championships for boys and girls at five age groups (under 16, 17, 18, 19 and 20) and has divided the country into four regions. The winners of the four regions meet to contest the national championships. There are also regional championships for younger boys' and girls' teams (under 12, 13, 14, and 15). Each state has a governing body (or two in the case of larger states) of youth soccer that is affiliated with USYSA. They often sponsor state championships for even younger teams, all playing an 11 v 11 format. In addition to sponsoring competitions for youth club teams, USYSA also administers a select program that is supposed to identify and train elite players.

The best players in each state can try out for state select teams (known as Olympic Development Program or ODP). The physical size of the United States creates a need for an efficient way to identify elite players, and the lack of experienced, well-trained coaches creates a need to concentrate the elite players. Players must be able to travel to, and afford the costs of, the often far-flung auditions and training sessions. Given the size of some states, a player might have a two-hour drive (or more) each way to train with the ODP team. These ODP teams usually train once per week, and then play in one or two regional tournaments which are used for selection to one of four regional teams. The regional teams are then used for selection of the youth national teams. The problem is that, even if the ODP has excellent coaches, they can do very little with the limited training time they have. The ODP does have the benefit of linking top players and should thereby improve the level of play. However, as the teams do not play together very often, the level of play does not improve as much as it could. Since so few players make it to the national teams, ODP is primarily a scouting tool for college coaches. Finally, as with any select program there are accusations of political influences on the selection process. In the end, ODP is marginally related to the Olympics or player development.

There are many varieties of soccer clubs in the United States. There are some clubs, such as the United German–Hungarian club in Philadelphia, that run similarly to European clubs. They have a men's team and a number of youth teams. For players under age ten, there is a league within their own club. There is a complex with a number of fields and a clubhouse with changing rooms and restaurant. Clubs of this type are the exception rather than the rule. There are few, if any, "football clubs" or "athletic clubs" as they are known in Europe. There is no clubhouse, or special club field.

Commonly, a youth team will form and then affiliate itself with a youth club. The teams therefore operate independently. Some of these clubs have technical directors or coaching directors who help train the coaches in the club. There are clubs, similar to the United German–Hungarian Club, that run in-house, recreational leagues of their own and sponsor select teams that are affiliated with outside leagues.

One club which has the full gamut of activities is Montgomery Soccer Incorporated (MSI) in suburban Washington, D.C. MSI runs an excellent program for five- and six-year-olds. It is a ten-week program that runs in the fall and spring. The first four weeks, the players have 30 minutes of instruction and then 30 minutes of play. The remaining weeks are just games. Each team plays two 4 v 4 games simultaneously (the squad is broken into two halves). The "referees" are high school players who have acted as their trainers earlier. Parents are required to stay at the ends of the field and at least ten yards from the field. If any parent or the team's actual coach gets too involved in yelling instructions to the players or keeping score, the referees are supposed to pick up the ball, stop the game, call in the coaches, and remind everyone that it is the children's game. At coaching clinics, the team coaches (usually parents) are instructed to talk with the players who are on the sidelines, the substitutes, and help them observe the game and learn from it. Scores are not kept and there are no standings. The players use size 3 balls and receive patches for participation. MSI then moves to 7 v 7 for seven-, eight-, and nine-year-olds, and then ten-year-olds and beyond play 11 v 11 (on either recreational or select teams). It is a well-conceived program which not only gives good experience to the players but also to the high school–age players who can try coaching. It is not uncommon nowadays in the U.S. to see young children playing small-sided games rather than 11 v 11. Even so, programs as comprehensive and developmentally appropriate as MSI's are rare.

There is a lot of variation as to how individual "select" teams run, even within the same club. In my experience, the typical "select" youth team plays 40 or 50 matches each year. Their schedule includes 18 to 20 league matches (half in the fall and half in the spring), state cup competition (part of the national championships at older age groups), and open tournaments. Teams usually train twice each week. There are at least three problems with this format. First, it means there are so many matches that training time is limited. Second, it overemphasizes the weekend-long open tournaments. As I will explain below, the tournaments are not an ideal learning environment. Finally, given the physical size of the country, it is difficult for top teams to play each other. Top teams win too much, leading to boredom and lack of challenge, and therefore lack of development, for the top players.

A team might enter four or five weekend-long open tournaments in a year. Often, a team might play five full matches in 48 hours. Such a packed schedule brings physical and mental fatigue that make learning and enjoyment difficult.

There is little emphasis on league play. A team must play in a league to be eligible for the state cup competition, which leads to the national championship. Especially for teams in the older age groups (under 19 and 20), leagues are a matter of convenience. In two states I know, the players return from college in the late spring, the coach re-forms the team, and they play in a weekend-long "league" to be eligible for the state cup. American youth teams rarely realize the developmental advantages of league play. These advantages include time for training and learning and the premium on consistency.

USYSA does not necessarily register every top youth player, but it does have most of them. There are some players in leagues not affiliated with USYSA. The allure of competing for a national championship and the chance to play with better players in the select ODP environment attracts the vast majority of talented young players. Even with the popularity of these programs, there are still stories of players who either did not know about them, could not get to the tryouts, or could not afford the fees. In many cases, these players are recent immigrants to the United States who are playing in the ethnic leagues of large cities.

Other programs for youth soccer players in the United States include school teams, soccer camps, and indoor soccer arenas. As players reach secondary school, they begin to play for their school teams in addition to their clubs (and ODP in some cases). School teams (and university teams also) have the advantage of being able to play or train every day, but the season is very short, approximately three months. School teams also play two or even three matches per week. With so many games in so short a time, it again means that training time is limited. It also means that from the ages of 14 to 18, top players are playing 80 matches per year with that many or fewer training sessions. During their high school seasons, those who play on club teams also are playing seven days per week without any chance for rest and regeneration. On the one hand, they are playing too much, and on the other they are rarely playing in a learning environment. With so many games in so short a time, it again means that there is little training time to review past performances or to correct problems.

There is also an issue of the role of soccer within many schools and universities. Because of the relative newness of the sport, few athletic directors are familiar with the game. Through a lack of familiarity, the sport often gets second-class treatment in an athletic department. Some administrators are openly hostile to the sport because they see it as a threat to their own favored sports (e.g. taking away athletes from American football). School and university soccer coaches often have to promote their programs within their schools.

Another aspect of youth soccer in the United States is the soccer camp. The best camps provide an opportunity for players to have fun and an intense week of playing. For kids who do not receive much coaching on a regular basis, the camps can expose them to ideas about the game that they won't otherwise see. However, a one-week "quick fix" will never make soccer players.

Indoor soccer arenas operate in many American cities. In areas of the United States that have long winters, these arenas provide youth teams with a chance to play. All of the indoor arenas with which I am familiar play indoor soccer with rules similar to hockey rather than *futsal* (indoor soccer as it is played in most of the world with boundaries rather than boards). The boards are in play and the ball is not weighted so that the game moves extremely quickly; the ball is like a pinball. The boards being in play mean that errant passes might still be effective. While the speed of play might be good for a player's technique, it is too fast for players to learn to make good decisions.

Because the United States is a large and wealthy country, facilities and equipment for youth soccer are rarely a problem. In some ways, there may be too much money in the game. Sporting goods manufacturers, seeing the socio-economic profile of the youth soccer-playing population (suburban, relatively wealthy), have actually helped turn soccer into an expensive sport in the United States. Youth soccer in the United States is full of conspicuous consumption in which many players feel they need three pairs of shoes, sandals, a leather soccer ball, uniforms just like the professionals, and a bag into which to put it all. Equipment costs, on top of fees for coaches, fields, tournaments, travel, ODP, and soccer camps, mean that one can spend thousands of dollars on youth soccer every year.

Facilities are a mixed bag. There is plenty of space, but the quality of the fields varies a lot. While there are a lot of "soccer parks" sprouting up around the country, the facilities vary widely. Many fields are overused, both by soccer teams alone and by other sports that may share them. Due to widely varying climactic conditions in many parts of the country, fields are difficult to maintain. Often fields are in parks where there are no changing facilities. While there are some difficulties, facilities and equipment are certainly available for youth soccer teams in the United States.

In the words of Graham Ramsey, coaching director of the Maryland State Youth Soccer Association (MSYSA), "There are two models of youth development in soccer. One is like they have in Holland where they have a well-conceived plan to nurture young talent through organized play at clubs and with well-trained coaches. The other model is the Brazilian one, where a majority of the population drops out of school at age 12 and plays soccer 18 hours a day in the streets."

In the United States, we have a society much like Holland's, but we seem to hope our youth soccer system will more closely resemble Brazil's. There are some valid reasons for the lack of an organized, disciplined approach. The United States is a large country. As the country has people from many different ethnic backgrounds, American soccer receives influences from many different approaches to the game. The sport is relatively new in the United States, so the structure of it is still evolving. Finally, the United States is a wealthy country. While soccer is popular around the world as the inexpensive sport of the working class, it is primarily a middle-class, suburban sport in the United States. Given this scenario, it is unlikely that kids will spend even one hour a day playing soccer on their own, when they have so many other options. Some of these options are good: school, homework, and other sports. Others can be less productive: television, video games, and the Internet. Given the size of the United States and the many options children have, youth soccer must be made as attractive as possible, as a source of fun and stimulation for kids.

PLAYER IDENTIFICATION

Identifying talent is crucial in any sport in any country. The greatest coach in the world cannot make a superstar out of just anyone. At the same time, recruiting can often take the place of training and coaching. At the youth level, concentrating solely on recruiting is not healthy. All kids can benefit from playing youth soccer. If a coach is willing to work with a player, he can help the player develop. If young players are cast aside, it is likely that they will harbor negative thoughts about the game. On the other side, the "stars" who are recruited often gain such a high opinion of themselves that they stop believing that they need to continue to improve.

The coaches who win the most in the United States are often the best recruiters. Since teams often spend so little time training, the only option for increasing the number of wins and improving their teams, as some coaches see it, is to go out and find better players. This recruitment often includes inducements such as paying for a player's equipment or excusing him from paying team fees. While European clubs offer inducements to players (such as providing their training gear and footwear), the inducements are the same for all of the players. The way it works in the United States can be unfair and yet another way in which too much emphasis is placed on winning and not enough on player development. I have seen teams that were supposedly inferior defeat teams that have been heavily recruited and full of so-called "select" players. Often, the losing coach's response was to go out and recruit more players for the next year. The players he had were full of potential, but he chose to replace them rather than try to train them.

It has also happened that a player joins a team in an area two or more hours' drive from his home. One former member of the United States Under 17 national team who lived in the Washington, D.C., area played on a club team in Philadelphia, 125 miles away. Even if he did go to training, the amount of travel time had to have an impact on his school work. As we will see in Chapter 4, European clubs are reluctant to take players from outside their immediate area unless they can put them in a boarding situation.

As mentioned above, there are often accusations of politics in the selection of ODP teams. These accusations only highlight difficulty in identifying *youth* players who show promise. Selection of players in the United States is entirely up to the individual team coach. College coaches are bound by the academic admissions standards of their schools. The freedom to find one's own players is important since recruiting is such a critical component of youth soccer coaching in the United States.

TRAINING TIMETABLES AND COMPONENTS

As mentioned above, elite youth teams usually train once or twice per week during the season. Because there are few dedicated training facilities, little practice time, and little time together away from the field, many of the coaches who possess some technical knowledge of the game do not have enough time to pay proper attention to the physical and psychological development a player must have. As the players age, a gap develops between European and American players in terms of psychological and physical preparation.

Youth soccer rules in the United States allow for players to reenter the match after they have been substituted. The effect of this is that games are played at a very fast pace. Players run themselves into the ground without thinking about where and why they are running. Of course, there are advantages to open substitutions. The first is that you can take out a player for a chance to talk with him about a certain aspect of the game and then put him back in to apply what you have discussed. Another one is that they keep all members of the team interested in a game, as they have a chance to enter or reenter the match.

COACHING

A great strength, and a great weakness, of American youth soccer is that there are a lot of volunteer parent-coaches with little or no experience in the game. It is a great strength because these people can bring a lot of energy, enthusiasm, and creativity to their coaching. It is a weakness because they lack experience playing, coaching, or even watching soccer. Therefore, they do not have a base of knowledge or full understanding of the game. While there are parent-coaches in Europe, they have grown up in countries where soccer has a primary sporting and even cultural role. Also, they tend to be in small, local clubs that are not on the main developmental track for professional players.

One way that USSF and the National Soccer Coaches Association of

America (NSCAA is not affiliated with the USSF) combat this problem is to hold very basic beginners' coaching courses which range in length from eight to 32 hours. These "crash courses" are an excellent idea for introducing people to the game and to coaching it. For example, the Maryland State Youth Soccer Association's eight-hour "Community" license introduces basic skills like running with the ball and dribbling. Someone who has been involved in the game his whole life is likely to have some knowledge on how a player should dribble the ball. Useful as the beginning level courses are, they cannot replace a lifetime of experience.

Another way to measure the quality of coaching in the United States is to consider the number of "serious" coaches. The NSCAA has 14,600 members[3] and holds an annual convention attended by more than (sometimes a lot more than) 3,000 coaches from the United States and all over the world. Members of this organization are people who take their coaching seriously. While the number of coaches who are members is large, it averages out to one "serious" coach for approximately every 200 registered players. The high ratio of players to coaches is one example of how we must manage the growth of the game.

Soccer has been popular in the United States long enough that there are people with experience in the game but they often choose not to remain involved in the game. For those with experience in the game who do stay involved, there are more advanced coaching courses. Both USSF and NSCAA offer a top course up to one week in length. These courses are significantly shorter than the top level courses in many European countries. For example, the top coaching course in the Czech Republic covers 450 hours, or nine full weeks, of instruction. The American courses therefore include fewer topics, and the topics that are part of the courses are not covered in as much depth. One earns a coaching license by successfully completing a coaching course. Few school or university coaching jobs in the U.S. require one to hold a coaching license. The European clubs that I visited all had minimum license standards for their coaches at every level.

Many coaches in the United States who do have experience can earn a lot of money coaching youth teams. Some youth teams will pay a coach $15,000 per year for coaching one team. Some coaches will "coach" five or six teams at the same time for the money. As the coach cannot be more than one place at a time, he or she must miss some games or training sessions or both. Therefore he is unable to make evaluations from matches or run properly planned training sessions. Some teams, desperate for a "big-name" coach, will have a practice coach (or "skills" coach) and a game coach. These two might talk on the telephone to arrange the team line-up but the one never sees the matches and the other never sees the practices.

Finally, these coaches with several teams have great difficulty building any kind of relationship with their players, so there is little loyalty to the team, and therefore to the sport. While it is difficult to begrudge someone the chance to make a living from coaching, if the focus is not on making better players, the system needs to be changed.

Due to limited training time (or to a coach who does not attend all the training sessions), there is often a lot of involvement from the coach during the match. While it is difficult to control one's enthusiasm for one's team, some youth coaches are constantly shouting instructions to their players. When coaches try to run the game, players, who are listening to the coach, do not learn to make their own decisions. Players who are concentrating on the game will not hear the coach anyway.

In most American sports, coaches have a lot of control during a game. They can call time-outs, decide on plays as in basketball or American football, or choose pitches as in baseball. Soccer coaches all over the world struggle with relinquishing control to the players during a game. For American coaches, it is especially difficult to allow their players to be creative and think for themselves for two reasons: First, as explained above, they have limited training time, and second, they live in a culture where coaches are allowed and even expected to make a lot of decisions during the game. The best coaches, youth or adult, train their players so that they are able to think for themselves and be creative in their games.

PHILOSOPHY

European clubs are trying to develop professional players for their first teams. The youth teams all lead up to the first team. That structure helps them to keep perspective on what they are doing. Winning takes a back seat to development as a player. At many clubs, developing a professional player means developing an individual whose personality will help him succeed as a player. The biggest contrast I saw between youth soccer in the United States and in Europe was in the philosophy of the youth programs. Since the philosophy dictates everything else, it is a vital area for coaches in the United States to consider. One can think of it as a question of ownership. Youth soccer in Europe is owned by professional organizations interested in maximizing their investment in precious resources (youth players that they want to develop for their first teams). Youth soccer in the United States is owned by the parents of the players. In American youth soccer, we must be aware of our different ownership structure and act accordingly.

Because of the wide range of youth soccer programs in the United

States, it is difficult to say there is a certain philosophy. USYSA has teams in such a geographically diverse area that any ideas the organization does pass down can take a long time to filter down to individual teams. If actions truly speak louder than words, observations of the behavior of the people involved in youth soccer give some indications about the philosophical aspects of American youth soccer. Having outlined many of the aspects of youth soccer above, one other group needs scrutiny: the parents of the players.

Adults, primarily parents, must be involved in order for organized youth sports to exist. I have terrific respect and gratitude for people who want to support their children by making it possible for them to play youth sports. My father coached, lined fields, set up goals, drove, wrote newspaper articles, bought fundraising items I sold and sold them himself at work, wrote checks, and many other things so that I could play youth soccer. However, parents can go too far. As I outlined above, many parents feel they must buy their children a lot of expensive equipment if they are going to fulfill their potential and win a college soccer scholarship. Parents also are too involved in other ways. I have seen parents carry their adolescent-aged children's bags to the field for them and even tie their shoes for them. As a parent myself, I have experienced (and succumbed to on occasion) the desire to do everything I can for my children. By doing too much of the arranging, we put our own needs ahead of theirs. We must remember it is the kids who come first. Not only are they the ones who have the fun and educational experience, but also they must learn to be responsible to the fullest extent they can be for their experience.

From the amount and type of influence that parents and coaches frequently exert and the youth game's structural flaws, it is difficult for many youth players to feel a sense of personal achievement in youth soccer in the United States. In the words of the father of one of my former players, "you can't caricature youth soccer parents." One example: late in a game, the coach takes out a goalkeeper who has played there all season to give him a chance in the field. The other team scores to tie the game, costing the team the league title. The parents surround the coach and scream at him. Later, they fire him. The players were 11 years old. Unfortunately, everyone involved in youth soccer has stories like this to tell.

As there is little account of the long perspective for developing top-class soccer players, youngsters see only external motivation: winning, gaining a college scholarship, and pleasing their coach. While these factors might be enough to keep them playing for a while, they will not keep players in the game for life. In my opinion, youth players rarely gain a sense of personal control in soccer. They do not have enough positive emotions associated with it. Even winning can feel very hollow when you have gone about it in the ways described above. As a result they do not continue in the game after adolescence as players, coaches, referees, or even spectators.

Some of the positive and negative features of youth soccer in the United States are summarized below.

SUMMARY OF YOUTH SOCCER IN THE UNITED STATES

Positives:
- High participation numbers.
- Parents are willing to help.
- Money is available, the U.S. is a wealthy country.
- Coaches' licensing programs exist, unlike any other sport in the U.S.
- Inexpensive (or should be inexpensive anyway).
- Safer compared to other sports, so that parents are willing to let their children try it when they might not let them try other sports.

Negatives:
- Owned by parents, not professional clubs, leading to an emphasis on short-term goals, rather than a long-term developmental program.
- Lacks a history of playing or watching. People don't remain in the game.
- The massive numbers of youth players have not translated into enough spectators to sustain a professional league. Even now Major League Soccer (MLS) is reportedly on shaky financial footing.
- The considerable growth in youth soccer has not been matched by growth in the number of adult players, coaches, or referees.
- Many parents and coaches lack experience in the game and there is a relatively small number of "serious" coaches. It means their efforts and money are often misplaced.
- Coaching courses are shorter, and therefore less comprehensive, than European coaching courses.

Some Questions About Youth Soccer in the United States

DOES THE CURRENT SYSTEM DEVELOP TOP CLASS SOCCER PLAYERS?

It is important to note that there have been some American soccer successes in recent years. DC United won the CONCACAF (Confederation of North, Central American & Carribean Association Football) Champions Cup and the Intercontinental Cup in 1998. John Harkes and Kasey Keller have won cup competitions with teams in England. Claudio Reyna has won the Scottish league with Glasgow Rangers. The United States defeated Brazil in 1998 and defeated Germany, twice, and Argentina in 1999, all in friendly matches. The United States' youth national teams have also had some good results in their world championships. However, these successes have not enabled the United States to produce enough top players to be competitive in the World Cup. The men's national team's last place performance in the 1998 World Cup Finals in France was proof that we are not producing top-class international players. American players with European clubs tend to sit on the bench at big clubs or play for mediocre clubs. During the 1999-2000 season in Europe, there were only a handful of Americans in the top divisions of the leagues in Germany, Spain, England, Holland, and Scotland. Perhaps further evidence of the lack of top players is that for the last two World Cups, we have imported "passport" Americans who have only let themselves be selected after it became clear that they were not going to play for their native countries. If the United States is going to be consistently competitive on the world stage, we must develop better players.

A related issue is that if we are going to develop top-class players, they need somewhere to play. Hopefully, MLS will continue to provide not only a place for American players to play and develop, but also a goal to which young soccer players can aspire. One of the problems with the development of top players in America is that top athletes pursue other sports with solid professional leagues that offer the chance of huge monetary rewards. For example, baseball superstar Nomar Garciaparra preferred soccer to baseball as a boy, but he could see that his prospects for professional play and pay were better in baseball. Curtis Pride, a member of the United States' 1987 Under 17 national soccer team, also elected to play professional baseball rather than pursue a soccer career. While we must prepare youth soccer players better, we must also be sure they have something to which they can aspire and somewhere to play when they are adults.

Finally, it is important to note that not every player can be a world-class or even professional player. In fact, one of the great attributes of the game is that one can enjoy playing it whether one is playing for the first or ten-thousandth time, whether one is fit or fat, or whether one is a professional or an amateur. Recreational soccer certainly has its advantages. Since its focus is primarily on having fun, it can keep perspective on such issues as development as a person and development as a player. Top players must come from a developmental system which makes demands on them to learn the game and work at it as hard as they can. In a highly competitive environment, it is difficult to keep balance between all the goals of youth athletics. Specifically, it is difficult to keep perspective on a youngster's developing as a player, having fun, and growing socially because a competitive environment implies concentrating on who is playing and who is winning. I would hope that we could create a system where more people become lifelong afficionados of the game, whether as coaches, referees, recreational players, or spectators. Our current system does not appear to be keeping people in the game. As pointed out earlier, the massive numbers of youth players have not lead to massive numbers of adult players (especially not top-class ones), coaches, referees, or spectators. For example, there has been growth in the number of participants in adult soccer leagues, but it has not been as large as the growth in youth soccer participation. The 1.5 million youth players in 1985 translated into only 175,000 registered adult players in 1995 (an increase from 103,000 in 1986).[4]

WHAT ARE THE IMPLICATIONS FOR AMERICAN SOCIETY FROM THIS TYPE OF SYSTEM?

I believe that top class players need not be created at the expense of having fun and learning about character. Keith Tabatznik, the Men's Soccer Coach at Georgetown University, once said to me, "That stuff [learning about character] is the most important at every level of the game." While I want to see the United States produce top-class soccer players, I want even more to see the products of youth soccer become adults who have learned the important lessons that youth sports can teach. Nowadays, with the distractions of television, video games, computers, and cars, youth sports are more valuable than ever for their positive impact on socialization and self-realization. While youth soccer currently does provide some of the physical and psychological/social developmental benefits that it should, it could provide so many more.

Most people would agree that youth sports are an excellent way for children not only to exercise their bodies, but also to learn social skills and find out more about themselves. Although this idea is difficult (if not impossible) to prove, studies that have been done seem to support it.[5] Because so many girls play soccer in the United States, I believe youth soccer has been particularly beneficial to them. My father coaches an Under 16 girls team that gets together on the night before games to paint their fingernails in the team colors. While this might seem trivial, doing something together is certainly a better alternative for them than watching television alone, or other unproductive activities. Certainly some of the benefits of youth sports are visible in American youth soccer.

In order to maximize their socialization opportunities from youth soccer, children must have time. They must have time to train, to play matches, to be around their teammates when not actively playing, to debrief, and to talk with their coaches, teammates, and parents. As I have stated above, opportunities to do this can be limited due to the nature of youth soccer in the United States. The basic problems are: coaches can have many teams which limits their time with each team; the ratio of training to matches is often low so teams are more often in performance mode rather than learning mode; and sports clubs are rare, meaning there is little time to "hang out."

Children will still grow mentally and socially, in some way, from what they experience and observe. Children see everything. The coaches and parents must try to ensure that the message is a positive one. As educator Marshall McLuhan pointed out, "the medium is the message." The American youth soccer system certainly sends strong messages to the children who participate in it.

If parents do too much organizing and equipment buying, players will gain a sense of entitlement that they have not earned. If coaches are missing games and training sessions to be with other teams or ranting and raving at the referee and the players, the players see that behavior. They receive a negative example of commitment, dedication, and behavior from the very person who is supposed to provide stability and leadership.

It is also important to think about whether youth soccer programs are using age appropriate activities. We can ask if youth soccer programs are developmentally appropriate for children in different stages of development: childhood, pubescence, and adolescence. While programs like Montgomery Soccer's, outlined earlier in the chapter, are terrific in that they account for developmental needs of the children, many other activities in American youth soccer do not do so.

For example, children up to about age 11 need to play exclusively in a learning environment, exploring the game while they learn the basic techniques. Many state youth soccer associations pile on the pressure by running state championships for teams with nine-year-olds. Eleven- to 15-

year-olds (those in pubescence) are often undergoing difficult changes regarding their bodies and attitudes as they come to understand the world around them. A lot of training and nurturing is what these kids need. Instead, the youth soccer system in the United States begins regional and national competitions, select teams, and more tournaments. School teams, too, begin at this age. There is a lot of activity and something at stake every time they play. Little thought, therefore, is given to development, and a lot of pressure is put on these kids which is exactly what they do not need.

The oldest group of 16- to 18- or 19-year-olds (adolescents) are often at the peak of their athletic powers. At this stage, one of four things happens. They are cut from their teams, they are burned out by too much competing previously, or they enter a college program where they only play four months per year and cannot fully develop their potential.

The final, and very recently started, possibility is for players to sign professional contracts out of high school. Some sign with MLS's Project 40 program and others have gone to European clubs. This option is encouraging, but it must be handled well by the players and the clubs with which they sign.

Another thing to consider is that children in the United States are unlikely or even unable to play on their own and so must be in an environment that encourages them to play. Of course, the coaches and parents creating the environment must be careful not to suppress opportunities for children to experiment with the game and have fun with it. However, they must give guidance so that maximum learning and enjoyment can be found in the relatively short times when kids are playing soccer. It is very difficult for parents and coaches to walk the fine line between providing opportunities and doing too much "hand-holding," but walking that line is the challenge we face.

It is not just in soccer or just in the United States that problems exist with the messages that children receive in youth sports. As I will discuss later, the youth directors at the clubs I visited in Europe think frequently about what messages their activities are sending to their players. Issues of character development in working with children are difficult to tackle for everyone all over the world. Therefore we should think about them and do the best we can to help players grow as people.

Conclusions

It is clear to me that the current system of youth soccer player development in the United States could work better. Because of the massive participation numbers and wealth of the United States, it may be that we will bludgeon our way to the top of the soccer world on sheer strength of numbers and money. I believe that it would be faster and more beneficial to society to do it with a better system of youth development, more thoughtfully planned and organized.

As the saying goes, "Think globally, act locally." This book is dedicated to looking at the ways in which youth players train. While there may be a need to change the policies of USYSA (for example), we can also change youth soccer one player or one team at a time. This book contains many ideas for those who work directly with young players.

The United States has plenty of youth players and playing facilities; they must be engaged more efficiently. There are many challenges to face for coaches and other youth soccer leaders in order to improve the youth soccer system in the United States. However, there are also many resources. Perhaps more than any other country. We must use them wisely in order to create a system that will hopefully turn out better soccer players and will also turn out people who have learned the lessons about life that youth sports were meant to impart.

As the youth soccer programs in European clubs are much older than those in the United States, we can learn from them. Not having a club structure like European countries is a difficult hurdle for Americans to overcome. Whether we develop a European-style club system or not in the U.S., there are things we can learn from the way European clubs operate their youth programs. We do need to pick and choose what we want in the U.S. and what we do not want. We cannot just copy the Europeans. In the final chapter, I will draw some conclusions about what we can implement from European youth training systems so that we can train better players in the United States.

Notes

1. Coaches' Manual of Eastside Youth Soccer Association, Bellevue, Washington: *http://www.eysa.org* (17 July 2000).

2. Statistics from the Soccer Industry Council Association of America (SICA) at *www.sportlink.com/research/teamsports/soccer/*participation/abstract96/index. html (17 July 2000).

3. National Soccer Coaches Association of America Web Page: nscaa.com (17 July 2000).

4. Statistics from the Soccer Industry Council of America (SICA).

5. Svoboda, Bohumil. "Sport and Physical Activity as a Socialization Environment." *Acta Universitatis Carolinae Kinathropologica* Vol. I, 1995.

Chapter 2

Organization, Facilities, and Equipment

At the end of the day though, it's really got to be up to the individual. They've got all the facilities they need here, so we're just trying to give them the right guidance and, most importantly, the right incentives.

— Dave Hancock,
Head Physiotherapist at the
Blackburn Youth Soccer Academy[1]

All over the world there are similar stories of many soccer clubs being started by groups of friends looking for a way to enjoy their leisure time. In order to have more regular games, teams banded together to form leagues. With regular league play, rivalries intensified and winning became more important. Also, as players specialized, people decided they would rather watch more skilled players than play themselves. A better team meant more spectators. When winning became more important, teams started to "hire" players. With professionalism, clubs started looking for ways to save money and still win. Eventually, they hit upon starting their own youth programs.[2] Slavia Prague, for example, has documents showing that the club had youth teams as early as 1910. The idea was that they would not have to pay transfer fees if they developed their own players. They also hoped that a player growing up in the club would have more loyalty to the club and desire to win for the club.

This brief history indicates where we have arrived today. Soccer is now a multi-billion dollar business around the world. For example, even youth teams' jerseys carry sponsors' logos. The organization, facilities, and equipment of top professional clubs' youth departments are a far cry from the "street soccer" that was played all over the world in years past.

There is no club system in the United States similar to the one in Europe. I include information about the background infrastructure of the clubs for three reasons: first, to give *context* to the player development activities (outlined in detail in later chapters) that the clubs undertake. Second, the information offers the chance to *compare* the European clubs' structures with what occurs in the United States (to show some of the advantages and disadvantages of the various systems). The youth sector organization in these clubs may provide some ideas we can use in the United States. Finally, description of the different European clubs' youth development systems can satisfy the *curiosity* of those who might be interested in understanding the structure of the European clubs' youth player development systems. While there are some interesting aspects to the organization, facilities, and equipment of the Europeans clubs for American coaches, these aspects are not as important as others, which I will review in later chapters.

Organization of the club is a question of the number of players, coaches and other staff, and teams. There are also more detailed descriptions of the teams. For example, how many coaches does each have and in what kind of league do they play?

One reason that soccer has always been so popular is that it is inexpensive. Nowadays, the top European clubs spend huge sums of money to provide the best possible training environment for their youth players. Many are building new *facilities* (like Blackburn Rovers', outlined below), buying all the latest soccer and athletic training equipment, outfitting their players in uniforms the same as the professional players wear, and sending their youth teams on trips abroad so that they can gain extra experience. The only required *equipment* to play soccer is a ball. Even that one critical piece of equipment can be manufactured with rags, newspapers, or old socks. Many of the world's greatest players learned to play on rock strewn "fields" with soccer balls made of such substances. Nowadays, those in charge of youth development departments must run them professionally, and they end up spending a lot of money.

In this chapter, I will present the basic structures of Newcastle United and Munich 1860 as examples of how these clubs organize their programs and what facilities and equipment they supply for their players. After the case studies, I will provide other unique and interesting ideas from the other clubs that I visited and the literature that I found. At the end of the chapter, there is a summary of the important elements of the European clubs' organization, facilities, and equipment.

Munich 1860 and the School Pilot Project

Some would say Munich 1860 is in a difficult position, as they play almost literally in the shadow of their city rivals, Bayern Munich. Bayern is one of the biggest and most successful soccer clubs in the world. Both teams play their home games in the Olympic Stadium in Munich, and their respective training grounds are about 500 meters apart. While I was visiting 1860, I saw their first team play Bayern and defeat them. It was their first "away" win over Bayern in 23 years. Perhaps it was an indication that 1860 is on its way. Being near Bayern is useful to 1860 in the sense that it gives them a clear measuring stick for the success of the activities in every part of their club.

Munich 1860's return to being one of the top teams in Germany has been long and hard. When the Bundesliga began in the early 1960s, it was 1860 that was in the first Bundesliga, not Bayern. After winning its only Bundesliga title in 1965, the team started on a downward spiral that eventually saw them relegated to the third division for financial irregularities. It took them many years to struggle their way back into the top flight. Now, 1860's Amateur, or reserve team, plays in the third division.

Munich 1860 has an impressively organized youth sector. The club's resources allow it to put into action a lot of ideas for different types of training. The club's budget for a year is *DM* 1 million (approximately $500,000). Bayern's youth budget is two to three times larger.

ORGANIZATION

The Munich 1860 Youth Sector is normally comprised of 12 teams, one for each year from ages six (Under 7 team) to 17 (Under 18 team). In the 1999-2000 season, they had an additional team, playing in the Under 16 category. This extra team was comprised each week of players from other teams who might not have played in their own teams' games. The reason that the extra team existed was that there was to be a new league the following year for the Under 16 level, and 1860 wanted to secure a spot in it without giving up the spots it already had.

The four youngest teams, Under 10 down to Under 7, play 7-a-side soccer across half of a regulation field. The goals are 18 feet wide × 6 feet high. The Under 7 players use a size 3 ball, and the other three teams in this group play with a size 4 ball. The teams play in leagues based in the city of Munich.

Munich 1860's older teams, from Under 18 down to Under 11, play regular 11 v 11 soccer with standard size 5 soccer balls. Because German youth leagues are organized for even-numbered teams (i.e. U18, U16, and so on), many of the 1860 teams are "playing up" an age group. The odd year teams (U17, U15, etc.) play in a league designated for older teams.

The Under 18s play in a league that covers all of Bavaria (the province in which Munich is located). It includes the junior teams from other professional clubs such as Stuttgart, Eintracht Frankfurt, and Bayern Munich. Instead of playing their home matches on the training fields of the club as the younger teams do, the Under 18s play their games at the 30,000 capacity Grunwalder Stadium 500 meters up the street. The Grunwalder was the home of both 1860 and Bayern until the Olympic Stadium was built. The winners and runners-up of the Under 18 league advance to a national championship. In the 2000-2001 season, a similar structure will be started for Under 16 teams, which is why 1860 has an extra Under 16 team this year.

There is also a German national championship for the Under 16 level. There is a provincial, or Bavarian championship for Under 14 teams. The Under 12 teams compete for a Munich area championship. The younger teams simply play their league seasons in leagues comprised of teams from the city. In addition to their league games, these teams play a number of friendly matches and travel to tournaments.

The Under 7 through Under 9 teams have one coach each. The Under 10 through Under 18 teams have two coaches. In addition, there are two specialist goalkeeper coaches who work with the different youth goalkeepers. There is a coordination/strength trainer who works with the different teams. There are also a number of physiotherapists to cover the youth training sessions and matches. In total, the youth sector has two administrators and two coaches who are full-time employees. There are also 20 part-time coaches.

FACILITIES

While 1860's current training facilities are very nice, they do not measure up to Bayern's. At this time, 1860's facilities include a building with the club offices and locker rooms. There is a small trailer that acts as the club shop. The first team and the Amateur team have their own grass practice fields. For the youth teams, there are two grass fields, an artificial turf field, and a small area for soccer tennis. The older youth teams and the Amateur and first teams visit a fitness center for weight training.

The club also leases space in a boarding house in Munich for 10–15 players. The players living in the boarding house are on the older youth teams. The boys in the dorm attend nearby schools. As it is expensive to rent the rooms as well as feed and care for the players, the club does not like to bring players into the boarding department unless absolutely necessary. Therefore, they must be top prospects if the club is going to spend the money to board them. This attitude may change when their new facilities are finished.

Construction will begin shortly that will make 1860's facilities almost identical with Bayern's. The first step will be to build a new building for the offices and locker rooms. This building will also contain a club shop, travel agency, and dormitory. The second step will be an indoor sports hall that will include a fitness center with weight training equipment and a full service restaurant. The final phase will be to upgrade the Amateur team's training field so that there is a running track around it. Ernst Tanner, director of 1860's youth sector, reported that the German Football Federation will soon require their professional clubs to have many of these facilities if they want to keep their licenses.

EQUIPMENT

Mr. Tanner is very pleased with the club's uniform sponsor, as it provides all of the players in the club with training and match kit. Players from the Under 13 team and older are provided with their soccer shoes. The Under 17 and 18 team players are limited to two free pairs each season; and after the first two, they must pay for their shoes. Mr. Tanner found that these players were abusing the system and not taking care of their shoes. His hope is that by limiting the free shoes, players will take better care of them. Each team seemed to have its own set of training discs (or cones), training bibs, and soccer balls (enough for each player to have one). The discs had small grooves in the top so that poles could be laid across two of them to make hurdles. This feature made them useful for coordination training.

LION SOCCER SCHOOLS AND THE SCHOOL PILOT PROJECT

All of the basic characteristics of the 1860 program are the same as those of Bayern Munich. The one big difference is that Bayern does not have an Under 17 team. Indeed, Mr. Tanner is considering having one squad of approximately 26 players to cover both the Under 18 and Under 17 teams. The reason is that by that age, the club has a fairly clear idea of how many of the players it will want to keep. To keep extra players just to make a team is both expensive and not fair to the players.

Munich 1860 is also involved in two programs outside of their regular teams. The first is what they call the Lion Football Schools (named for the club's mascot). These are essentially clinics held throughout Bavaria and even in Austria for boys from 9 to 15 years old. The *fussball schule* meet once per week for interested players. 1860 is serious about training these players, and the schools can be used as a scouting mechanism. However, the club started the program in order to get involved in the community and to win back fans after its long struggle to return to the top level of German soccer. The second special program is known as the School Pilot Project.

An interesting and unique program in which 1860 participates is their School Pilot Project. 1860, Bayern, Unterhaching (the third Bundesliga team in Munich), and the Bavarian Soccer Federation cosponsor the Project. 1860 and Bayern do all of the funding. Coaches from the three Bundesliga teams in Munich work with players in the Project so that they can receive regular, expert coaching. The training has three focus points: technique, coordination, and small-sided games. The organizers include the small-sided games in large part to keep the enjoyment in it for the players. The school groups are not teams and do not play matches. As the players in the program are from several different clubs, tactics are not part of the training.

As the Project was new during the 1999-2000 season, it encompassed soccer players in fifth through seventh grade at three schools. The sponsors were working on plans to expand the Project for younger kids in primary schools. The current schools are three different types, so that the Project can reach students of all academic levels. It is the same at all three schools, so that should a member of the program need to switch schools, he will be able to remain in the program. The schools were chosen for their location; they are near the training facilities of Bayern and 1860. Basically, the five training sessions in school amount to an expanded physical education program (see Figure 2.1). The students in the Project have three soccer specific training sessions each week at school. The other two sessions are called "Sport Basics": areas such as swimming, athletics, and coordination training. The final part of the Project is that 1860 and Bayern share the cost of a bus which picks up the boys at their schools and delivers them to their clubs for training in the evening. In addition to their school activities, the players at this age usually train three times each week with their clubs. A side benefit for the clubs is that they can monitor the education of their students.

Time	Monday	Tuesday	Wednesday	Thursday	Friday
7:55–8:40	German	Math	Soccer	Soccer	German
8:40–9:25	Math	German	Soccer	Soccer	Math
Break					
9:45–10:30	Sport Basics	Science	German	English	Social Studies
10:30–11:15	Sport Basics	Social Studies	English	Religion	Music
Break					
11:35–12:20	English	Religion	Science	German	Sport Basics
12:20–1:05	English	Music	Math	Math	Sport Basics
Lunch					
2:05–2:50	Art	Soccer	Homework	Homework	
2:50–3:35	Art	Soccer	Shop	Homework	
3:35–4:35	Homework	Homework	Shop		

Figure 2.1. Sample Schedule for a Player in the School Pilot Project

The School Pilot Project has a unique audition. All boys who are interested can attend open tryouts in the spring of their fourth grade years to enter the Project the following fall as fifth graders. Fifth and sixth graders can also try out to join the program, although few do. Since 1860 and Bayern pay for the Project, they have the option of placing their players directly into it without auditioning. All the players who are auditioning play in small sided games and are observed doing ball manipulation (fakes, feints, and juggling). In addition they go through a number of skills tests. There are three different tests that involve the boys moving through some kind of agility exercise and then either shooting or heading a ball on goal. There is also a test in which the player moves toward goal, playing wall-passes off of benches and then shooting. The final test is a 20-meter sprint. In each area, except the sprint, they are rated from 1 (best) to 6 (worst). From the open tryouts, some boys are brought back for a second round of auditions before the coaches make selections as to who will be in the Project.

In terms of the number of teams that they have, the facilities that they provide, and the equipment they use, Munich 1860 is representative of most of the teams that I visited. What makes their program stand out is the School Pilot Project and their proximity to their arch rivals.

Summary of Organization, Facilities, and Equipment at Munich 1860

- Munich 1860's organization is typical of many clubs in Europe. They have teams for each year from Under 8 up to Under 18. The younger teams play 7 v 7 and the older teams play 11 v 11. The leagues in which the teams play cover expanding territory. The rules are adjusted slightly for the youth players.
- The club has a training center with a number of fields and is about to begin adding to them by building a gymnasium and fitness center.
- The club has a sponsorship agreement with a uniform supplier that enables them to outfit all of their players with training wear, uniforms, and shoes. They also have plenty of training bibs, cones, balls, goals of various sizes, and athletic training equipment.
- 1860 sponsors a School Pilot Project in conjunction with Bayern Munich. Many of the club's players participate in it. The program enables the club to give young players extra training during the school day.

Newcastle United FC and the FA Academy Scheme

Newcastle United, located in the northeastern part of England, is in a good position for developing top-class soccer players. The area around Newcastle has long been known as a hotbed for talented players. Jack and Bobby Charlton, Paul Gascoigne, Peter Beardsley, and Alan Shearer are just a few of the many stars who have come from the area. The club is also in an advantageous position because its popularity with supporters and the wealth of its owners mean that it has the resources to invest in a good youth policy. Indeed, they spend approximately £1 million ($1.6 million) per year on youth development.

Organization

The Newcastle United Academy has ten teams, encompassing approximately 148 players. The teams range from Under 9 up to Under 17 and then skip to Under 19. The English Football Association (FA) has established an Academy League for the age groups Under 9 up to Under 19. All of the teams are sponsored by professional clubs. They compete in geographic groups, playing some intersectional games, during the season that runs from the end of August to the beginning of March. At the beginning of March, there are play-offs involving all of the teams, which culminate in the crowning of national champions in each age group. The Under 9 through Under 11 teams play 8 versus 8 on a 60 yard by 40 yard field. They use a size 4 ball and small goals (6 feet high and 18 feet wide). Before matches, the coaches of the two teams agree on how many periods will make up the game. For example, they might play three 20-minute periods or four 15-minute periods. They play more than two periods so that they can talk more with their players about what is occurring in the match. It is also easier to send players in and out of the matches since the coaches can allot them periods, rather than running them in and out during play. There is a clear emphasis here on the matches as learning experiences. The older teams play the traditional two halves and use size 5 soccer balls. The games increase in length as the players grow older.

The activities of Newcastle's youth department run in accordance with the guidelines of Football Academy Scheme of the FA. Each club in England can make some of it own independent touches in how its Academy is structured, but the FA determines the bulk of the structure.

One of the reasons the FA has the Academy program is to ensure that there is a minimum standard of youth-player training in the country. Therefore, clubs in England must apply to the FA for permission to run an Academy if they can provide the requisite facilities, coaching, and other amenities.

Newcastle has only Under 17 and Under 19 teams. Most academies seemed to have the same arrangement. To have more would be logistically difficult, and it is unlikely they would be able to bring so many players through to their first team. Between the Under 19 and the first teams, there is a Reserve team.

Additional facilities must include: an outdoor artificial field, an indoor playing area 60 × 40 yards, locker rooms, study area for 40 students, a parents' lounge, computerized registration and student records, email and internet links to the FA and the league, and a junior football center providing regular football for 100 nonregistered students under the age of ten.

The reason for the recruiting radius at the younger age groups is that the FA do not want boys to miss school to attend club activities. Also, they expect to have Academies set up all over the country which will have roughly equal facilities and coaching so that there will be no need for boys to travel long distances in order to find top quality training. The reason that the radius restriction is removed for older players is that many of these players have left school, and many of them are already professionals.

Table 2.1
Requirements of the FA for Youth Football Academies[3]

Age Group mum Length of ing Sessions Week	Field Space Minimum Number of (in yards) Games Allowed in One Season	Maximum Number Maximum of Players in Each Recruiting Age Group Radius	Mini- Coach- Each
under-9 to (in 2 sessions) under-12 under 12) (4 age groups) (all small-sided — 8 v 8)	1 area 60 × 40 for Minimum 24 each 40 players Maximum 30	40 Within one hour's travel of the club	3 hours (except
under-13 to Minimum 24 under-14 sessions) (2 age groups under 12)	1 area 60 × 40 for Within one and each 30 players Maximum 30	30 a half hours' travel of the club	5 hours (in 3 (and
under-15 to Minimum 24 under-16 sessions) (2 age groups)	1 area 60 × 40 for Within one and each 20 players Maximum 30 travel of the club	20 a half hours'	5 hours (in 3
under-17 to Minimum 24 under-21 Maximum 36 (5 age groups) (including internationals)	1 full size field No Restrictions	15	12 hours

Football Academy Staff must include: a full-time Academy Director (Alan Irvine in Newcastle's case), a full-time Assistant Academy Director for Under 9 to Under 16, a full-time Assistant Academy Director for Under 17 to Under 21, a full-time physiotherapist for Under 17 to Under 21, a physiotherapist for Under 9 to Under 16 who is present whenever they are playing, a full-time Education and Welfare Advisor, an on-call doctor, a specialist goalkeeping coach, and a sufficient number of coaches so that there is one coach for every ten players at every coaching session.

It is important to note that the Under 17 through Under 21 players fall into two categories: those on scholarships and those who are professionals. In addition to their 12 hours of football training, the scholars must participate in 12 hours per week of some type of learning program. It can be academic or vocational. While the scholars receive a nominal weekly stipend, the professionals receive a regular living wage.

The club is required to hold two in-service workshops for the coaches each year, and the FA also conducts two. The club's workshops tend to be specifically on technical football training, while the FA's are on various topics such as conditioning, psychological training, and other topics related to training.

In addition, the FA provides numerous bureaucratic guidelines about the procedures and timing for signing, retaining, and releasing players, the minimum age of players, renewing an Academy's FA approval, and codes of conduct for the Academy.

In total, the Academy's technical staff includes three full-time administrators who also coach, 20 part-time coaches including specialists in goalkeeping and conditioning, a scouting director, and two full-time physiotherapists.

FACILITIES

Eventually, facilities and equipment at all English Youth Football Academies should be roughly equal. Since the Academy concept is only about three years old, clubs are working toward completing campuses for their Academies. At Newcastle United, it is a time of transition for all of the facilities. In addition to the expansion of their main stadium, St. James' Park, the club is also trying to build a dedicated training center. While the club owns the property and has blueprints ready, they are awaiting city council permission to start work. So at this time, the club's training activities are farmed out to several different facilities. The first team and the reserves train at a sports center in a town outside of Newcastle. The Under 17 and 19 teams train at the University of Durham outside of Newcastle.

The remaining youth teams train at three different sites within the city. Due to the current situation, the club transports many of its players from St. James' Park, in the city center, to the training facility in Durham. While these facilities are spread out and not specifically designed for Newcastle's needs, they do meet the FA's criteria for a Football Academy. For example, at the University of Durham, there are dining and changing facilities, a gymnasium, a weight room, a running track, an artificial surface field, and more than five grass fields. The school that the players attend for the academic part of their scholarships is across the street. While not convenient to the Newcastle city center, the complex does have a lot to offer, particularly privacy and good athletic facilities.

EQUIPMENT

Availability of proper equipment is not a concern for the coaches. All players are provided with training and match uniforms that are identical to those worn by the first team, including the logos of the sponsors. In addition, the older players receive two pairs of soccer shoes (one with molded studs and one with screw-in studs) at the beginning of the season with the opportunity to replace them as needed. The younger players take care of their own training uniforms. The coaches have at their disposal plenty of balls, cones, training bibs, goals of various sizes, and other athletic equipment. The only time there is a worry is when the laundry delivery to the training ground is late, delaying the start of coaching sessions.

SUMMARY OF ORGANIZATION, FACILITIES, AND EQUIPMENT IN THE NEWCASTLE UNITED YOUTH ACADEMY

- The English FA dictates through its Football Academy Program many of the guidelines that affect how Newcastle runs its youth program.
- The FA requires clubs to have high standards in their youth academies, but in almost every case, Newcastle exceeds the requirements of the FA. For example, the coaches usually have higher coaching licenses than demanded by the FA.
- Newcastle's youth teams play in leagues sponsored by the FA and containing teams from other top English clubs. The rules are modified for the youth players. Reentry is permitted and they play three or four periods in a game.

- The club does not have a dedicated training center but it is building one. All of the facilities it does use meet FA standards.
- Newcastle provides its players with all of their training equipment, match uniforms, shoes, and even meals. In short, the club meets all of their playing needs.

Ideas from Other Clubs

As one can see from just these two clubs, their organizations, facilities, and equipment are roughly equal. What makes these two stand out is that Newcastle is part of the FA's Youth Football Academy Scheme, and Munich 1860 participates in the School Pilot Project. Below are some unique and interesting ideas from the other clubs that I visited and about which I read.

FC BARCELONA

FC Barcelona, or Barça, spent more money on its youth program by a wide margin than any other club that I visited. Annually, they spend 1.2 billion pesetas (approximately $8 million) on their youth teams.

The youth program at Barça starts for players who are only six years old. Each year approximately 1,000 boys from the ages of six to eight try out to be members of Barcelona's "Football School." The director and his staff of six select the top 200 boys. At this level, the parents of the players who are selected pay a nominal fee for their children to be part of FC Barcelona. The School is run within the club; they do not play outside opponents. Each team trains for one hour per week and then plays in a "social tournament" each Saturday. The format is 7 against 7 (six field players and a goalkeeper) on fields that are 60 meters by 40 meters. The players use a size 4 ball. The goals are smaller than regular size, 6 feet high and 18 feet wide. They play only on the dirt fields in the "City of Barça," the area around the club's main stadium.

One reason Barcelona spends a lot more money than the other clubs that I visited is its dormitory for youth players, La Masía. Currently, 46 boys live there. The boys living at the residence are mainly from regions of Spain outside of Barcelona but there are also boys from several other countries. They attend local schools and the club provides language instruction for those who need it. The club provides a teacher who helps the boys in the dorm with their lessons.

GLASGOW CELTIC FC

Celtic runs eight football centers throughout Scotland for ten-year-olds. These players play with their own teams, but come to train with a coach from Celtic once or twice per week. They also play matches approximately once per month. The club's scouts use the centers as a vehicle to scout players for the club's Under 12 team.

Underlining Celtic's commitment to youth development is the fact that they spend £1.6 million ($2.6 million) on their youth program each year. This figure includes the nominal wages that the full-time youth players receive and the costs for the Under 21/Reserve team. Some of that money goes toward providing their players with equipment. When a youth player joins Celtic, he can sign in two ways. Younger players sign a Developmental Form, or D Form, which means the club pays for the players' footwear as well as their training and match uniforms. The Schoolboy Form, or S Form, provides all of the benefits to the player of the D Form and also a nominal wage to the player (e.g. £10, or $16, per week). The club coaches use the S Form as an incentive for the players.

Celtic has a state-of-the-art fitness center in their stadium. The weight machines, treadmills, and other equipment are interesting. From the Under 16 players up to the ones on the first team, every player has his own key, which contains a computer chip, for the equipment. Each machine has a screen that displays the individual player's workout when he inserts his key. After the workout, the fitness coach uses the keys to download the players' workouts into a computer. In this way, the coaches can ensure that the players' workouts are designed correctly and that the players are doing them.

Celtic also employs the full array of staff to support the work of the players and coaches. As with other clubs, Celtic has several physiotherapists to ensure that youth training sessions are covered by one of them. There is also a nutritionist, a strength/conditioning coach, a physiologist, and a sports psychologist. These people work primarily with the full-time players (Under 16 to the first team) but they are also available for the other coaches to consult. The expertise of these people, combined with the state-of-the-art fitness and rehabilitation equipment at the club, ensures that Celtic's coaches stay abreast of developments in all areas of football training.

SK SLAVIA PRAGUE

In contrast to the other clubs that are profiled in this chapter, Slavia Prague does not spend as much money on youth development. This is not by choice, but by necessity. The economic circumstances in the club are such that the club can afford no more. Indeed, even without spending so much money on their youth development program, their program is just as comprehensive as the other clubs'. They spend approximately 4 to 4.5 million Czech crowns (approximately $100,000) on their youth sector each year. While this is very little compared to the budgets of the other clubs reviewed in this chapter, it is a lot by Czech standards. Sparta Prague is the only other club in the country that spends as much as Slavia. A dollar goes a lot farther in the Czech Republic than in countries in Western Europe.

There are several ways in which Slavia saves money. One is that the club does not provide footwear or training uniforms for its youth players. Players receive tracksuits only. The players are responsible for providing the remainder of their gear. The club does not have the money for a lot of fancy athletic training equipment. When they do physical training, they do a lot of exercises using their own body weight, medicine balls, and handweights. The handweights are old water bottles filled with sand. Another way in which the club saves money is that there are no physiotherapists for the youth sector, but the club does have access to a doctor for consultations if a player is injured. Similar to other clubs, all of Slavia's youth teams travel extensively to tournaments throughout Europe, both during the winter break (the weather in the Czech Republic necessitates a three-month break in the league schedule), and after the season in June. Also due to the club's financial situation, the players usually split the cost of traveling to tournaments with the club.

During the 1999-2000 season, the sports bodies and government in the Czech Republic reintroduced a sports elementary school program that existed during the communist era in that country. A soccer club must sponsor the school, providing coaching and money. The Czech ministry of education also helps with money. Boys in the program must be part of the sponsoring soccer club (in this case Slavia). There are 50 schools in the Czech Republic that have soccer sponsors. Clubs in other sports have similar relationships with elementary schools. If a boy should leave the club but is interested in remaining in the program, Slavia allows it as long as the program is not oversubscribed and the boy's behavior is acceptable. Boys who attend the school but do not play for Slavia can also be part of the program if there is room. Eighty to ninety percent of Slavia's 9- to 14-year-old players are in the single sports school that the club sponsors. The school is across the street from Slavia's training complex. The program covers grades three to six and is being expanded to grade seven. The program includes five hours of physical education each week. Two of the hours are for regular physical education classes. The boys attend swimming class during one hour. The final two hours are back to back so that there is time for a proper soccer training session. This basically amounts to a fourth training session for Slavia's teams (as they train three times per week after school). During the winter, the coaches use the two-hour session for other activities like gymnastics, basketball, and handball. While Munich 1860 and its partners go into schools to administer their program, Slavia essentially has its own school.

The club does not undertake any regular pattern of helping boys with their studies, but does help those who need it on a case-by-case basis. It is different than most clubs since the majority of the club's youth players in the "pupil" categories attend the same school. It makes it easy for the club to maintain a relationship with the school and the teachers in it.

AFC AJAX AMSTERDAM

The many books and videos about the Ajax youth system highlight its reputation as a top club for youth development. Ajax has turned their home-grown talent into four European Cup titles as well as numerous Dutch championships.

One difference from other clubs at Ajax is that all of their teams have 16 players except the Under 16's, "because there are a lot of problems with the growth spurt and the differing levels of strength, so there are a lot of injuries. There are 20 players on this team."[4] Johan Cruyff, when he was head coach at Ajax, advocated a slightly different system. He wanted to create a third Under 16 team (instead of two) at the club. He believed that with growth differences at that age, some talented players were left out simply because they were not big. By creating a third team for smaller players, he believed they might give a chance to smaller players who needed more time to grow.[5]

At Ajax, the club has recently built a new training center for their youth players which has been dubbed "The Future." "To compensate for the loss of street soccer in the busy city of Amsterdam, [they] have developed a soccer playground for the youngest Ajax players. Twice a week the 8- to 12-year-olds can enjoy themselves there, playing soccer tennis, header volleyball, keeping the ball in the air, or small sided games. The soccer playground underlines the Ajax philosophy that young players cannot spend too much time with the ball."[6]

Former director of the Ajax Youth Department Co Adriaanse adds, "We have rejected the idea of putting all our talented youngsters into the same school. It is essential for the development of a child's personality that he should be allowed to grow up in his own environment. This means with his own family, in his own street, with his own friends, and at a school of his own choice."[7] And he stresses, "All of the boys live in the neighborhood and go to school here so we pick them up from school at two o'clock, bring them here and they train for an hour and a half. Then they eat and do their study here. We have 14 teachers to help them with their education, and all the lessons they would normally miss that afternoon at school they do here, and then they train here until 7:30 P.M."[8]

BLACKBURN ROVERS FC

Blackburn, in England, has built a state-of-the-art training facility for their youth players. It includes a two-tier swimming pool (you can walk in the water in one half and swim in the other), a three-quarter length artificial field and a short sprint track. Outside, there is another track, a special goalkeeping area and a sprint hill. There are also four full-sized fields. The cost of the training complex was £7.5 million ($12.5 million).[9] The club's head youth physiotherapist, Dave Hancock, summarized: "At Blackburn Academy, the players receive a full-time education on every imaginable football topic, from sports psychology to dealing with the media, as well as having a choice of college courses."[10] Training elements are covered in detail in Chapter 4.

Conclusion

Organization was roughly similar in all of the clubs I visited and about which I read. Some clubs had more or fewer teams, coaches, or special programs. The organization is important primarily in that it represents a certain philosophy of player development. The philosophy of the youth programs is the topic of Chapter 6. There are three key elements in the clubs' organization that I believe are important. First, the structure building up to the first team makes it easy for everyone involved to keep a healthy perspective on player development, rather than winning. This arrangement gives European clubs a significant advantage over American ones in the development of players. Second, the youngest teams play 7-a-side until the players are nine or ten years old. By keeping the numbers down in matches, every player is more involved in the action in each game. The third interesting aspect of the clubs' organization is the school programs which Munich 1860 (with Bayern Munich) and Slavia Prague administer.

There is currently a lot of attention surrounding the *facilities* clubs are building to support the work of developing their youth players. The facilities at Ajax, Blackburn, or any other club, are merely venues for developing players. The clubs really do seem to have everything the players need to train. Dave Hancock, the head physiotherapist at the Blackburn's Academy, concluded, "If they can't make it here, with the facilities we've got, they won't make it anywhere."[11] I think that his comment misses the point. While facilities such as Blackburn's are certainly nice and undoubtedly helpful to training, nice facilities alone do not make players. There are many stories of players, all-time-great players, learning the game in total poverty, wearing soccer shoes and using a real ball for the first time when they signed a professional contract. If anything, the clubs are offering their players too much. Providing too much must be part of the clubs' worry about the right guidance and incentives for the players. Hopefully the guidance also involves excellent training in the game. The facilities, organization, and equipment are not as important as *who* uses them (i.e. coaches and players) and *what* they do with them (e.g. interaction, learning, types of training).

Equipment also was roughly equal in all of the clubs which I studied. No team which I saw train lacked for enough balls, cones, bibs, goals, or other materials. The only equipment I had not seen before was the marking discs with grooves in the top. The grooves were the right size to hold poles so that the discs could be used to make mini-hurdles. Most of the players were outfitted as well as the first team in their respective clubs. I agree with the Newcastle coaches who were concerned that they were *providing too much* for their players. Slavia Prague was an exception, spending far less than most of the other clubs on their youth program. The players wear their own clothes and soccer shoes to practice. So many great players in the history of the game have come from so many different backgrounds that the equipment they had as youngsters must count for very little.

Organization, facilities, and equipment are all noteworthy components in developing top-class soccer players. Of course, in each of these areas, if they are handled properly, there can be benefits to player development. At the same time, good or bad, they are not critical factors. There was enough variation within the clubs I saw to indicate that there are many ways to handle each area. Also, top soccer players have come from every conceivable background: different countries, cultures, and socio-ecomonic classes. In our effort to develop as many top-class players as possible, we should strive to provide the best organization, facilities, and equipment for developing players. One caveat to this attempt is that it is possible to provide too much for youth players, that they can be too comfortable.

Regardless, from my observations, the areas in this chapter are not as important as some others. Of course, the players do learn from their environment and the organization in which they work. A club's philosophy of youth development colors how it selects players and coaches and how the two work together in training. Therefore, the philosophy is important in determining how a youth program is organized so that it sends the best message to the players. While the areas in this chapter are important, it is critical that coaches identify youngsters with potential and desire and work with them in the right way to develop their potential. These four critical issues (Player Evaluation, Training, Coaches, and Philosophy) are the subjects of the next chapters of this book.

Notes

1. Massarella, Louis. "The Water Boys," in *FourFourTwo* #68, April 2000. Haymarket Specialist Publications Limited, Teddington, Middlesex, England, p. 101.

2. Szymanski, Stefan, and Tim Kuypers. *Winners & Losers: The Business Strategy of Football.* Viking, London. 1999, pp. 3–4.

3. *The FA Premier League Handbook, Season 1998-99.* FA Premier League Ltd., London, 1998, pp. 49–60.

4. Allen, Matt. "Doing It for the Kids," in *FourFourTwo* #66, February 2000. Haymarket Specialist Publications Limited, Teddington, Middlesex, England, p. 95.

5. Barend, Frits, and Henk Van Dorp. *Ajax Barcelona Cruyff: The ABC of an Obstinate Maestro.* Published by Bloomsbury, London, 1997, pp. 35–36.

6. Kormelink, Henny, and Tjeu Seeverens. *The Coaching Philosophies of Lous van Gaal and the Ajax Coaches.* Published by Reedswain Videos & Books, Spring City, PA, 1997, p. 76.

7. Kormelink and Seeverens, p. 74.

8. Allen, p. 95.

9. Massarella, pp. 100–1.

10. *Ibid.*, p. 100.

11. *Ibid.*, p. 101.

Player Evaluation

The difference between making and not making it is so small....
But then you go back to what is professional football and what is
beautiful football. And then you understand that footballers who
have a little less don't succeed because their speed of action is too
slow, or their technique is a little less, even though when they stand
still maybe they're very good technically. Then it's about vision and
other things.... [There are] very good players. But at a certain
moment, it has to be done quicker, where instead of having two
meters to control the ball you have half a meter, and if the ball
moves half a meter you've lost it.

— Johan Cruyff[1]

Coaches in every sport must choose which players they are going to
train. Of course, they want to choose the best players. While American
coaches are not scouting European players, the processes that European
clubs use and the criteria they look for in players can help American
coaches to evaluate talent.

In this chapter, there are detailed descriptions of the scouting systems
at Munich 1860 and Slavia Prague. As these clubs are at opposite ends of
the economic spectrum, they provide some interesting contrasts as case
studies. After the case studies are sections on the different aspects of player
evaluation. The sections include information from the other clubs that I
visited and ideas from coaching literature. There are five sections: the system of scouting and signing players, the characteristics that clubs want in
a player, the methods of evaluating and retaining players already in the
club, the release of players, and the success of clubs in developing players.
I will consider each of these areas, both in the two case studies and in general. At the end of the chapter are a summary and conclusions about the
evaluation of youth players in Europe.

Munich 1860: "A Typical Munich Club"

Because 1860's city rivals Bayern Munich is one of the biggest clubs in Europe, if 1860 sat back and let players come to them, they would lose out on the best players to Bayern. Kids are lining up to play at Bayern. The German league is very competitive. While Bayern may be ahead of the pack, there are a lot of clubs right behind them. In Germany, there are several clubs in which the youth training opportunities are approximately equal. Therefore, the club must be very active in looking for talented young players or it will fall behind its rivals.

When I asked Mr. Tanner, the youth director, about their player recruitment, he said 1860 was "a typical Munich club." When one is competing with Bayern Munich for players, "typical" means more active than it might in other places. While 1860 does have access to a boarding house, the vast majority of its players still come from the city of Munich. There are some from as far away as Austria. The club has found it difficult to bring in youth players who do not speak German or understand the culture and so, while they consider these players, unless they are exceptionally promising, they do not take them into the club.

The club does have a network of scouts and Mr. Tanner goes out himself to look at players. If the scouts like a player, he goes for a trial at 1860 that usually lasts several weeks. The trialist trains with the club's team in his age group. If the player does well in the trial, he will sign and the club will set the wheels in motion for his transfer. The player might start with 1860 right away or wait until the start of the next season.

Unlike the trials for the School Pilot Project (see Chapter 2), 1860 does not ask players on trial to go through any skills tests because they have a chance to view them for several training sessions. At the trials for the School Pilot Project, there are hundreds of boys to see, and some form of special testing makes the process more efficient.

As in some other countries, 1860 must compensate the clubs from which it takes players. If the player comes from another club, and all but the youngest do, the base transfer fee is *DM* 3500 (approximately $1750). It goes up depending on how many appearances the player has had for his club, regional, and national teams. The maximum is *DM* 5000 (approximately $2500). Mr. Tanner reported that the club has spent *DM* 100,000 (approximately $50,000) in the last few years acquiring players.

When the coaches select players for the youngest teams at 1860, Mr. Tanner warns them that they must select players whom they believe can be in the club for several years. He sees the cruelty of cutting seven- and eight-year-olds and dashing their enthusiasm at such a young age. He also added that he would be just as happy to drop the programs for the youngest players. The problem is that amateur clubs will not give up their 10-year-old players without a fight, so that 1860 must start earlier than age ten if they are going to be able to attract top players. He added that only the big clubs can pay transfer fees for ten-year-olds. This situation is bad in two ways: it concentrates all the best players in one or two clubs so that youth matches are not competitive, and it seems crazy to pay money for a player so young. Buying kids like commodities can mean we start to think of them as such.

The coaches meet with the players (and their parents in the case of the younger players) three times per year to review their progress: at the end of preseason, at the end of the fall season, and at the end of the spring season. In this way, players are aware of what their strengths and weaknesses are and where they stand in the club. The players and their parents have some preparation in case the club is going to release the player.

Boarding is one of the perks the club uses for its players. Mr. Tanner only wants to spend the large amount of money to board a player if he is highly promising. Indeed, some of the players that the club boards pay their own boarding expenses.

When 1860 does have to drop a player, at any age, they help the players find another club in which to play. The players usually do not return to their original clubs. Once they have had a taste of the "big time" atmosphere, they want to try to continue with it. In the words of Mr. Tanner, "They would see returning to their home clubs as a personal defeat." They usually switch to other clubs that play in the same leagues as the 1860 teams. Mr. Tanner added that while some players who leave the club do improve and go on to become professionals with lower-division teams, none have improved to the point where the coaches wanted to take them back into 1860.

For players who finish their youth careers with 1860 as Under 18s, there is some good news. From the 1998-99 team, all of the 16 players on the team signed professional contracts for the following year. Five are with the 1860 Amateur team, which plays in the German third division. During the season, two of them have moved into 1860's first team squad. One other player went to a third-division team. Four players signed with fourth-division teams and the final six with fifth-division teams. Mr. Tanner said that it was standard for all of 1860's Under 18 players to get some kind of offer from a professional club, although it was a particularly good year for players to remain with 1860 by moving into the Amateur team.

While there are only two current members of 1860's first team who went through the club's youth program, Mr. Tanner believes the number will go up in the coming years. He believes the club will produce more of its own players because it has placed renewed emphasis on its youth section in the last five years and it has not taken full effect yet.

SUMMARY OF PLAYER IDENTIFICATION AT TSV MUNICH 1860

- The scouting system at Munich 1860 is straightforward. There are scouts who are on the lookout for players. Initial reports on individual players are usually followed up by Mr. Tanner himself, and he is part of the final decision whether to bring a player to the club.
- Unlike 1860's School Pilot Project (see Chapter 2), 1860 does not ask players on trial to go through any skills tests. Mr. Tanner did not mention any specific characteristics that the club's scouts look for in a player. A number of coaches in the club told me activity and aggression are important traits. They want players who get involved. Of course, technical and athletic abilities are also important.
- The coaches meet with all players three times each year to review their play. The club provides extra support (e.g., boarding or working with the individual trainer if necessary) to players whom it values highly.
- The club helps players it releases find new clubs and usually has no problem finding them one. Players who make it through the 1860 system are able to continue their soccer careers at some level, if not at 1860.
- While the club has only two players from its youth program in the first team at this time, they expect that number to grow.

SK Slavia Prague: The Big Fish in the Small Pond

The story of Slavia Prague closely mirrors the history of its country. The club was founded in 1892 from a debating society whose main agenda was Czech independence from the Austro-Hungarian empire. Slavia's jersey (half red, half white, with a red star on the crest) is a reproduction of the flag of Czech independence from that era. The club enjoyed great success during the inter-war period when Czechoslovakia was truly independent. During the communists' reign of the country, Slavia was forced to change its name several times and took a backseat to two other teams in Prague: Dukla (the army team) and Sparta (the communist party team). Since Czechoslovakia's independence from the Soviet Union in 1989 and the Czech Republic's split from Slovakia in 1992, Slavia has enjoyed success again. In the last ten years, they have made several runs to the quarter-finals and semi-finals of UEFA competitions. In recent years, the Czech championship has usually been a two-horse race between Slavia and Sparta. In 1996, Slavia won its first Czech championship since 1937.

1860's youth budget is five times larger than Slavia's. Money goes further in the Czech Republic, however, since prices are generally lower for everything. Slavia is one of two premier clubs in its country while 1860 is one of many clubs at the elite level in Germany. Slavia may be a big fish in a small pond, but there is still quality in the pond. The Czech Republic has far fewer citizens than Germany so that the talent pool is smaller. Since Slavia has fewer resources with which to work, they must be efficient with them.

Due to Slavia's status as one of the two biggest clubs in the Czech Republic, it is common for youth players to contact the club. Most of Slavia's players come to the club after they have first contacted the club asking for a trial. The club reviews the player's credentials. If the player's experience looks promising, the club sends someone to observe them with their teams, then decides whether to have them in for a trial. There are three other ways that the club scouts players. First, when their teams play games, the coaches keep an eye out for talent on the opposing team. Second, especially for the youngest teams, there are open tryouts, which the club advertises for in the newspaper. Finally, the club's coaches have gone out to scout players at the schools. The club has curtailed this program because it was not fruitful. A few years ago, they went to fifty schools and looked at over one thousand players. They brought in approximately sixty of them for trials, and none of them was selected for Slavia teams. To make such an effort and not find any players seemed like a waste of time.

Slavia does want to scout players in the whole of the Czech Republic, but they have found that there are not enough good players outside of the Prague area to make the effort worth it. The vast majority of their players come from the greater Prague area. Typically, they have 15–20 players from their total of approximately 160 living in a dormitory. Most of the boys in the dormitory come from towns near Prague, but far enough away that the daily commute to training would be too time-consuming for them to attend school, do their homework, and attend training.

The coaches at Slavia do not have set criteria in mind when they evaluate a player. The different coaches are often looking for different characteristics. For the younger players, it is easier to use set criteria. Ludek Prochazka, the club's youth chief, mentioned four traits the club's scouts seek in young players: speed, activity, courage, and awareness. He added that in his experience, differences among players in these areas remain (approximately) the same as they age.

When a player comes in for a trial period, it usually lasts two or three weeks. During that time, the player trains with the Slavia team in his age group. After the trial, the Slavia coaches decide if they will keep the player or not. If the player is going to join the club, he can start with Slavia right away.

If they do decide to keep the player, they must work out an arrangement with the player's former club. There is a transfer fee structure for youth players in the Czech Republic. For eight- to ten-year-olds, if there is a transfer fee, it is very low. However, the club that the player is leaving must agree to his leaving. For 11- to 14-year-olds, the basic fee is 10,000 Czech Crowns (approximately $260). For 15- to 18-year-olds, the basic transfer fee is 30,000 Czech Crowns (approximately $780). The players' home clubs are free to negotiate for more money based on a player's appearances with national teams or other honors. They can also put in a clause that Slavia will pay more money if the player makes it to Slavia's first team. If Slavia and the other club are not able to come to some arrangement, there is a tribunal at the Czech Football Federation that mediates disputes. A team can only lose two players per year. Even if Slavia is offering a lot of money, the club can say no to a transfer if they have already had two players leave that year. Mr. Prochazka said that the transfers are rarely a problem because the players want to come to Slavia. While the players do not officially have the right to change clubs on their own, in practice they do because the clubs can't hold back players who don't want to play for them.

The squad size of Slavia's teams steadily decreases as the players age. There are approximately 30 players in the youngest age group (for two 7 v 7 teams). At the oldest age group (Under 18), there are only 16 on the team. The club usually releases players at the end of the fall season (there is a three-month winter break in the Czech season) or at the end of the spring season. Even if a team adds a player during the season, it does not mean that the team will drop someone else right away unless they are over the roster limit set by the league in which the team plays.

When players are released, the club usually has no problem finding another place for them to play. Sometimes, when a player joins them, his old club will ask for the right of first refusal if the player is released. Due to its elite status in the country, other clubs are often interested in Slavia's players if they are released. Usually half of the Under 18 team will move into Slavia "B" (the reserve team, which plays in the Czech third division) the following season. The remaining players are able to find other clubs if they want to continue their careers. For the vast majority of Slavia's players, the B team is as far as they go with the club. From the B team, players often leave for other teams in the lower divisions. In the 1999-2000 season, the club had only two players on its first team who had played for Slavia as boys. While the club does turn out professional players regularly, they hope to turn out more players for their own club in the future.

SUMMARY OF PLAYER IDENTIFICATION AT SK SLAVIA PRAGUE

- As the club cannot afford a large scouting system and it is one of the biggest clubs in the Czech Republic, Slavia usually waits for players to come to them. When they receive a letter about a boy, they check his experience and go out to scout him.
- The club does not have set characteristics that it seeks in a player. Mr. Prochazka said that in his experience speed, activity, courage, and awareness are important. They are important because the differences between players in these categories remain the same through the years.
- The players have regular meetings with the coaches to review their performances. The club has little material incentive to induce players to stay, but their prestige within the Czech Republic is usually enough. The club has lost youth players to foreign clubs.
- Players are released at the end of the fall season or at the end of the spring season, unless adding a new player during the season puts the club over the roster limit. Players who are released have little trouble finding another club. Each year, about half of Slavia's oldest youth team joins Slavia's reserve team for the following season. The other players are able to join other clubs if they want.
- While Slavia has turned out many professional players, they have not been as successful in developing players for their own first team.

Scouting in Other Clubs

FC BARCELONA

Barcelona begins talent recruitment in its "football school" for six- and seven-year-olds. From this intramural program, the club selects the players for its youngest competitive team for the following year. Other new players come from a large talent scouting operation. The club utilizes 15 scouts in the region of Catalonia, another 15 scouts in the rest of Spain, and ten more scouts scattered throughout the world.

According to Spanish law, a player is free to change clubs up to the age of 14. However, Barça contacts the boy's former club anyway and offers them some fee. The fee also will increase should the boy someday make it to play for Barça B or the first team. Players from 15 years and older belong to their clubs and Barcelona must pay a transfer fee, just like they do with professional players.

FC Barcelona also has a developmental agreement with 15 local clubs. The affiliated clubs help with scouting and might take a player who is not quite ready to play for Barça and work with him in the hopes that he will improve. In return, Barça provides these affiliated clubs with money, technical advice, and coaching clinics. These affiliated clubs also can take on players who do not make the grade at Barcelona. Barça also runs leagues for teams affiliated with their fan clubs, or *peñas*, which take place on their dirt training fields. Working with the peñas is a good way for the club to build good relations with its supporters and could be used as yet another scouting mechanism.

Barcelona also has *two* Under 21 teams (Barça B and Barça C) so that players are able to stay on longer there than at many other clubs. The Under 21 teams play in the third and fourth divisions respectively so that when a player leaves them, he already has experience playing against professional players, making him more attractive to other clubs.

Glasgow Celtic FC

Celtic employs a large scouting network, based primarily in Scotland and Ireland. In this day and age, agents and the Internet also play a role in player recruitment. Mr. McStay, Celtic's head youth coach, receives a large number of letters and e-mails every week. He responds to all of them. While I was at Celtic, there was a player there on trial whom the club gave the chance based on the recommendation of his agent.

After each Under 18 game, Mr. McStay writes a report on his team which he reviews in a meeting with the club's general manager. The report includes a general report on the game and the team's activities and then one or two lines on each player.

Newcastle United FC

The way the club tries to predict which players have a chance to be pros is not science, but there are certain qualities for which they look.

Awareness, technique, and *athleticism* are the first characteristics they look for in a prospective player. They want to know if a player can see the game around him and act accordingly. Of course, it is also important that he be able to control the ball. They also want a player who has good physical tools. *Attitude* is another important attribute. As any coach would, Newcastle coaches and scouts are looking for players who listen and work hard. Alan Irvine, the Newcastle Youth Academy Director, also mentioned *aggressiveness.* By this quality, he did not necessarily mean physical aggression, but an aggressive attitude: to attack when you have the ball or to take on a defender 1 v 1. Scouts are always looking to find better players than the ones currently in the club who might be later bloomers.

With the recruiting radii enforced by the FA (see Chapter 2), the club must look locally for young talent. Younger players must live within one hour's travel of the club and older players within one and a half hours. Some English clubs are avoiding these restrictions by helping a young player's family move into the club's area. The oldest players at Newcastle can, and do, come from all over the world (although primarily from Great Britain and specifically the Newcastle area). The Newcastle area has traditionally been breeding ground of professional players. Alan Irvine believes that since regional economic differences have decreased and all of society is more affluent than it once was, being in Newcastle is not the advantage it once might have been. Newcastle's chief youth scout Peter Kirklee disagrees. He thinks many top players are still growing up in the area but that until recently they were going to other clubs for their apprenticeships. Both men agreed that Newcastle's youth program had been rejuvenated in the last few years, reaching the latter stages of the FA Youth Cup among other achievements. The rejuvenation has meant they are able to attract more local players. Regardless, the club is looking for the best talent it can find, wherever it can find it.

Having looked at how some big European clubs evaluate talent, we can consider talent identification more generally. While the clubs described above have a lot of good ideas about scouting, theirs are not the only ones. There are other good ideas regarding the system a club uses to scout players, the traits a club looks for in a player, the methods a club uses to evaluate and retain its own players, the ways in which a club releases players, and how successful the clubs are at identifying talent. The following sections review each of these areas.

Scouting Systems for Players

A club's scouting system can be organized many different ways. There are certain principles that must exist in any successful scouting system.

There are four key criteria: simplicity, accuracy, efficiency, and productivity. According to English coach Malcolm Cook,

> the scouting system must be simple in design and be relatively easy to administer and record. The scout should ensure that [a report] is as accurate as possible and keep to the objective without allowing other factors to get in the way. The scouting system should not involve the scout in the time-consuming chore of sorting out a mass of sheets, symbols or figures. Instead it should concentrate on the areas that really matter and record them effectively. [Finally,] no matter how good the assessment looks or how much time has been spent on producing it, it must help [the club to identify players with potential].[2]

Bayern Munich has a simple method of seeing a lot of players at one time. In cooperation with the club's uniform supplier, Bayern holds its own tournaments, which reap two benefits. In addition to publicity, the club gets a good look at almost 3,000 eager youngsters. To date, seven of these tournaments have taken place; the latest, held in early April 1999, yielded four more players for Bayern's youth development program.[3]

For the wealthier European clubs, scouting is a world-wide operation. In fact, some clubs have affiliated youth clubs in other countries. For example, Ajax Amsterdam and Manchester United have youth training centers in South Africa. West Ham United (from London, England) has one in Sydney, Australia.[4] At Ajax Amsterdam, they bring in non–Dutch players for trials at all ages, but they cannot sign them until they are 16 years old. The club has found that integrating foreign youngsters in the youth set-up often causes problems due to their lack of familiarity with the local culture and language. Ajax also has a very specific system of play, which takes time to learn. Foreign players stay at the club for a minimum of two years so they have a chance to learn the language, the culture, and the way of playing.[5]

Coaches and scouts with whom I spoke agreed that the older players are, the harder it is for them to break into a top club's youth program. Some said that, on physical abilities alone, it was difficult for new players at the older age groups. The fitness and coordination training at top clubs is so intensive that players who have not been in as intense a system will struggle. Mr. Tanner at Munich 1860 added that they are likely to struggle because their technique and reading of the game are also not as good.

Johan Cruyff, who was a great player at Ajax Amsterdam and Barcelona, later returned to those two clubs as the coach. In a 1997 interview, he said that if he were still in charge at Ajax, he would involve former players, current coaches, and scouts in decisions on players.

Let's say there were 100 boys at the end of one of the selection gatherings and all the leaders were there. With me, leaders had an enormous influence where youth were concerned. Because they are around those little guys for the entire week, the whole year. And they always know what the quality is and what's there. Because they see them every week. They're our automatic quality control meters. I think they should have a lot of influence.

Imagine that at a certain moment you had one of those gatherings where the boys show how good they are. One of the trainers—it doesn't matter which one — says: "Why don't we have that kid back?" And I say: "Have that kid back? He hasn't touched the ball." And he says: "That's why! Has he not touched the ball because he can't play? Or because he's so good at finding space?" Yes, they could both be true. So why send the kid away? Yes, let him come back. If it turns out later he's no good, well OK. But it's not proven yet. It only shows that everything is possible. I think at the moment that there aren't enough people who would dare to say that.[6]

Johan Cruyff's comments provide some insight into how difficult it is for a scouting system to run smoothly. His comments also show that it helps to have a lot of people involved in the decisions and to be organized.

Player Characteristics

Top class soccer players come in all shapes and sizes. There are also degrees of speed, strength, quickness, and other physical abilities among elite players. World-class players also run the gamut of personalities. Children grow at different rates and players improve at different rates. Therefore, it is extremely difficult to know what traits to look for in a youngster that might indicate he will develop into a professional player.

As there are so many attributes to consider, the key question is actually what characteristics do scouts and coaches consider most important? Generally, they want to pick players with characteristics that they feel they cannot train. While every player can improve in every aspect of the game, every player also has limitations. As Mr. Prochazka from Slavia put it, differences between players in certain areas when they are eight years old remain there when they are 16. Perhaps his evaluation shows a need for more individualized training. Among the clubs that I visited, the attributes that scouts and coaches wanted, that they felt they could only improve marginally, included: athleticism (particularly speed), an aggressive mentality, awareness of the game around them, and technical ability with the ball. They felt they could help players improve in these areas but that they needed a strong base from which to start. Identifying the key attributes of a youngster is an area of much discussion and research.

Scientists are looking at ways they can help identify young players who have the potential to be professionals. There is no clear consensus regarding the relative importance of scientific measures (see Figure 3.1) in predicting soccer talent. However, scientific profiling can generate a useful database against which talented players may be compared in order to identify potential strengths and weaknesses. These measures can also be helpful to scouts and coaches in confirming their initial perceptions of a player's strengths and weaknesses. While such profiling may be used for the purposes of picking players one might not otherwise have picked, the use of such measures for *not* selecting players is questionable and unethical.[7] There are at least two reasons not to eliminate players based on scientific measures. First, the scientists have not tested their hypotheses fully. Second, a player can be a bad athlete and still be an effective player. Gerd Muller is an example of a player who might not measure up to scientific evaluation, but was one of the most effective players in the history of the game.

Figure 3.1 summarizes potential areas in which scientists can play a role in evaluating youth players.[8] Most youth coaches do not have access to scientists. At a minimum, the predictors in the figure are useful for coaches as a way to organize their thoughts as they evaluate a player.

From the different sports science disciplines above, scientists have found some tests to be predictors of football talent. It is difficult, if not impossible, to measure some of the potential predictors. "Culture/Nationality" is not only difficult to measure but also likely to be a prejudiced analysis. All types of players have come from many different countries and cultures.

Two scientists, Mark Williams and Tom Reilly, compared groups of "elite" and "sub-elite" players over the four disciplines in the figure above. The tests included 15 anthropometric measurements of their bodies such as height, weight, and skinfolds (body fat measurements). They gave the players some tests of aerobic and anaerobic fitness, speed, agility, and power. They also tested the players' psychological profiles. Finally, the players went through some soccer-specific skills tests. From their research, the scientists concluded that the four biggest factors separating the two groups of players were: *agility, speed, motivational orientation* (task oriented as opposed to ego oriented), and *anticipation skill*. While the "elite" players scored significantly higher in almost all of the tests, the four above stood out the most.[9]

While the results above may prove useful for scouting purposes, there are three caveats: first, they can only be used to complement subjective evaluation from soccer experts (coaches and scouts). Second, they should

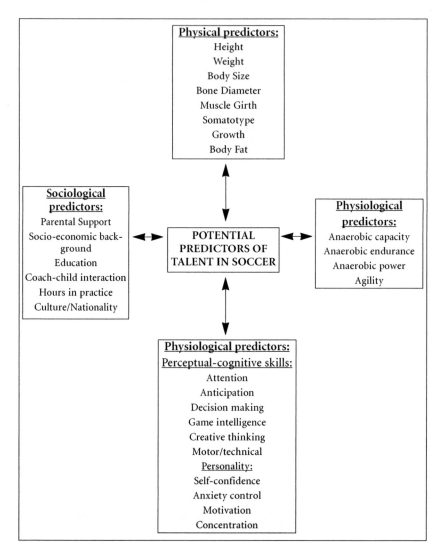

Figure 3.1. Some Potential Predictors of Talent in Soccer from Various Sports Science Disciplines

only be used for selecting in someone who you might not have chosen otherwise. There is not enough scientific data to say with certainty that players who do score well in the tests should not be selected. There is also a lot of anecdotal data about "late bloomers" or players with poor athletic ability who became top players. Third, without a longitudinal study of whether the "elite" players in the studies made it as professionals, the results only compare players at different levels of youth soccer, not players at different levels of youth soccer who *made it as professionals.*

Many clubs and coaches use their own selection criteria. Many variations are available. Using a standard format helps to keep records and to compare one player to another. Clubs can keep information from scouts so that they can build up information on players and clubs for future reference.[10] The Fulham FC assessment form (see chart below) is only one possibility to show how clubs rate players who have trials with them. All of the clubs that I visited made a point of talking with trialists about their evaluations. The coaches from the club wanted to be sure the trialists understood why the club would sign or not sign them.

Player's Name :	
Age group : Under __	
Group Coach :	
ASSESSMENT	
Performance and understanding of:	ASSESSMENT MARK
1. Passing and Control	A B C D
2. Dribbling & Turning Techniques	A B C D
3. Running with the ball	A B C D
4. Finishing Techniques	A B C D
5. Heading ability	A B C D
6. Understanding of the game	A B C D
(offense/defense in Small Sided Games)	
7. Attitude to coaching & practice sessions	A B C D
8. Competitive spirit & enthusiasm for match play	A B C D
9. Speed & Agility	A B C D
Overall Grade for Trial	A B C D
Additional comments:	
Signed _____ (Group Coach)	
KEY TO GRADES	
A = Above group standard	
B = Group standard	
C = Some weaknesses (monitor)	
D = Not at required standard	

The Fulham Academy Trialist Assessment Form (U9 to U12)[11]

Craig Simmons, the Player Development Advisor to the English FA, provides the following guidelines for prediction of soccer potential in a player (he did not specify a certain age):

- Individual technique qualities
- Opposed skills — a player's level of understanding of his role in the action of the team.
- Playing position effect — how does the player's position affect his performance: is it a position he usually plays? Does he play many positions or just one?
- Age — with children, one year is a big gap in ages. Players in the older half of the selection year tend to dominate selection.
- Body Size
- Maturation — Some children finish growing at age 14, others at age 20.
- Growth Changes — Many children undergo "awkward stages" during growth periods.[12]

He concluded with remarks about self-concept in children:

> The development of self-concept is a commonly overlooked aspect of childhood and adolescence. It is often affected by the child's level of biological growth and maturation.... Some children maturing later in their year group occasionally demonstrated anxieties and a lack of confidence if struggling against older and bigger opposition. However, as they grew and were matched effectively with suitable opposition "the catch up characteristic" created an improvement in their game and improved their confidence. The early developing and bigger boys occasionally experienced the opposite effect, this being early success with confidence diminishing as the physical dominance reduced. This period of transition demanded a degree of understanding and reassurance that all the growth factors would even out in adulthood with the players' continued learning of techniques and football intelligence being the key to long term success.[13]

When Johan Cruyff returned to Ajax as the coach, he had a lot to say about the youth program there. In 1981, he said:

> Over the last few years in Holland and also at Ajax we selected far too much for physique. Ajax has only two B-junior teams, teams for 15- and 16-year-olds. So what have I seen? Players of 14 who came from C to B who were sent away because they weren't physically strong enough. At that age youngsters are still growing and you shouldn't send them away, especially those players who are technically good. You should develop a third B team for small players who can develop further. I was too small myself when I

was 14 or 15. Small people have two advantages: because they are small, they have to watch what's around them on the pitch and they have to be quick because otherwise someone will walk all over them. So their vision is very well developed. Secondly, someone who's technically strong but physically weak is usually two footed.[14]

He used the example of Dennis Bergkamp, a star of the Dutch national team and one of the best players in the world during the 1990s.

> I've never been involved in discussions about numbers 14, 15, or 16 (the bottom three players in a team) because it's pointless. But you do discuss numbers 6 and 7, because they're the people about whom you're thinking: can he do it, or can't he?
>
> At Ajax, the opposite happened. Bergkamp was rejected every year because, as a right winger, he was in the second team. He really would have been kept there. No-one knows why. It's really inexplicable that two or three people said: "Why don't you let him go? He's such a shy boy." Because if he gets through and let's say he becomes really fanatical, the chances are that he'll become a very good player.
>
> Another example who was kept because of the system — or really was taken on because of it — is Aron Winter [a regular member of the Dutch national team through the 1990s]. I think he was also turned away four times. And one trainer disagreed with that and said: "I want to take him to an international tournament because I'm convinced he can do it." And I said: "If you're convinced, you must take him with you, and if you think he should stay at Ajax, then he should stay. I'll give him a year. We'll see. If you're convinced, of course, I'm 1,000 percent against sending someone away."[15]

It is clear that age is a factor in player selection. At Newcastle, the majority of their players are born in the first several months after the September 1 age-group cut-off. A few years ago, the birth date cut-off for youth teams changed from August 1 to January 1. Slavia Prague tried to keep the same cut-off and thereby play their younger players against other clubs' older ones. While they did get the competitive matches they wanted, they found their older players (ages 13/14 and older) were developing bad habits because they were so overmatched physically. They were playing with fear of being injured and kicking the ball just to get rid of it. The English FA has run a special boarding school for elite youth players for many years. "Over 50 percent of players who attended the FA's National School at Lilleshall were born between September and December (September 1 was their birth date cut-off), whilst a similar percentage of players selected for the England national team during the 1986, 1990, 1994, and 1998 World Cup qualifying campaigns were born early in the selection year."[16] The players who are slightly older as kids are likely to be bigger or more physically developed and therefore more likely to be selected. Early selection means better training so that, as the saying goes, the rich get richer.

West Ham head of youth development Tony Carr said: "All you can look for is instinct; natural talent and enthusiasm for the game. You look at a boy and ask questions, such as: Is he quick? Has he got good ball control? Is he a dribbler or is he a passer? We just look at their raw natural ability. We just look at any player who has a natural talent for the game and over the course of a few years we try to work out what his best position might be. I don't think you can spot a striker at eight years old, only a good footballer."[17]

Ajax head of youth development Hans Westerhof stated: "We look for technical skills and speed. Everything is based on skill, not strength or height, because it is not easy to develop. We only scout attackers. Let's say we scout four players for the left side. The best will be the winger, the second in midfield, the third in defense, and the fourth on the bench. After the ages of 15 or 16 we sometimes look for defenders, but at the beginning you have to have technical skills and speed."[18] At Ajax, there is also an emphasis on quality. In one season "only 14 seven-year-olds matched the criteria, even though Ajax scouts observed thousands of [youngsters] during the so-called talent days on location at youth soccer clubs in the region and ring the weekly matches played by youth soccer clubs."[19]

Ultimately, clubs and their coaches must prioritize the many traits they want in a player. It is unlikely they will find the finished article. Also, while science may eventually aid in selecting players, coaches and scouts will always be the ones who will ask the basic question, "Can this player *play*?" In Chapter 7, I will discuss the traits I think are most important in a youth player.

Player Evaluation and Retention

Just as schools give out report cards so that students know how they are progressing, coaches must give evaluations to their players so that they know how they are progressing and where they stand in the team and in the club's future. For example, at Glasgow Celtic and Munich 1860, the coaches meet with each player (and his parents in the case of younger players) three times each year to review his progress. At the same time, the club must make certain moves to retain the players in which it sees promise.

At Ajax Amsterdam, "In principle, an Ajax youth player is only a member for one year. An average of 30 of the 160 youth players drop out after one season."[20] All teams must decide how to evaluate their current players to decide if they still see them as potential professionals or if they believe they can replace them with better players. Ongoing evaluation is also important for the players so that they know where they stand; if they need to improve their efforts or prepare to find another club. At Ajax, "Twice a year, in April and December, the [evaluation] report is discussed with both the player and his parents."[21] The "report card" contains grades in the following areas:

- Ball control, dribbling, passing, beating an opponent, shooting, speed of action, attacking headers, scoring ability, crosses, speed on the ball;
- 1 to 1 duels, defending, defensive headers, sliding tackles, tackling, attacking the ball;
- combination skills, overview, positional play, adherence to assigned tasks;
- athletic personality, speed off the mark, speed from 0 to 10, from 10 to 30, and above 30 yards, mobility, strength in the tackle, stamina, running skills and jumping power;
- charisma, leadership ability, match mentality, attitude towards others, teammates, coach, referee, etc., receptivity to coaching, and ability to withstand pressure;
- other information: modest, cheeky, creative, plays in the service of others, character player, technical player, right footed, left footed, two footed.

The players are rated on a scale of 1 to 9 for each element.[22] "These assessments result in one of three recommendations: A — stay, B — doubtful (B/A doubtful/stay), C — go (B/C doubtful/go). The Head of the Youth Department makes the final decision which is then communicated to the player (in the case of those players under 15, their parents are also present)."[23]

Johan Cruyff has some thoughts on this topic also. In a 1981 interview, after he had started coaching at Ajax, he said,

> I've advised the board to stop signing youth [players to professional] contracts. Don't give a boy of 17 a [professional] contract. They should be happy they can learn something at Ajax. In principle, you should keep a 17 year old with the A-juniors, and sometimes let him play in the C-team (the second team), and if he does well there, sometimes he'll go on to the first team

so he can get a taste of the atmosphere. If he doesn't understand it and plays badly in the C-team — and by that I don't mean that he fails to beat his man or someone passes him — then you put him back, and not to A-1 but to A-2. He still has a chance. I think the young are getting tougher mentally. When he's 18 you can say "he's done it" and you can pay him back for those years.[24]

Bayern Munich has a similar concept. Their youth players receive allowances of *DM* 200 to 300 ($100 to $150) per month. Wolfgang Dremmler, Bayern's director of scouting, says, "We don't want them to go down that financial road too soon, otherwise they develop the wrong priorities. If a player is good and proves he can contribute to the club, then he'll get plenty of opportunities to earn money later on."[25] Glasgow Celtic also provides some of their players with a weekly stipend so they have a little spending money. The stipend is held up to the players as an incentive.

From the clubs' perspective, being able to retain their players is an important issue. If they are going to invest a lot of money in developing youth players, they want to be able to ensure that they can reap the benefits of these programs. At Blackburn Rovers in England, players who have left school to play full-time must commit to the club for three years. The club signs those with the greatest potential to six-year contracts.[26] "Mike Bateson, then chairman of Torquay United a [English] club that oscillated between the Second and Third Divisions, said, 'I'm damned if I'm going to put my money into a youth system just to let the bigger clubs snaffle up the product.'"[27] It is a concern for all clubs that they be able to retain the players they have worked so hard to develop.

Releasing Players

Releasing players is always difficult. It can signal to a boy that it is the end of his dream to be a professional soccer player. Especially in the highly competitive environment of soccer in Europe, clubs must seek out the best talent they can find. Inevitably, players will be dropped by the wayside. As indicated in the previous section, clubs meet with their players for performance reviews. One of the reasons for this is that it reduces the shock factor when players are released. There are other important issues in how a club releases a player. Do they help the player find a new club? Have they provided him with another option if it is the end of his soccer career?

At Ajax, "the most stringent selection criteria are applied to the players in the second year of the Under 14 level. Young players who leave Ajax still head the scouting lists of other clubs, and are much sought after. Ajax does not exclude the possibility of their return at a later date."[28]

While Co Adriaanse was at Ajax, he did not accept players falling by the wayside as inevitable. As he put it, "I sift through all the details, looking for causes, and consider what conclusions I should draw, in terms of making changes to scouting and internal selection."[29] Surely one of the reasons that Ajax does have a record of producing top players is that there is a system in place not only to evaluate their players but to evaluate themselves, to see if they are choosing the right players and training them in the right way. For this purpose, data on all their own players as well as the many players they scout are kept in a computer database.

At some point, the developmental clock simply runs out of time. It is difficult to say when this is. In every sport, there are famous "late bloomers" but at some time, the club must start to look to younger players. In 1993, Johan Cruyff gave his opinion, "You can see the signals that Wijnhard (an Ajax player) plays in the second team, and he's also 20. And he's not going to get into the first team. As a 20-year-old he's either too old for the second team or he should be in the first team. It's one or the other."[30] Ludek Klusacek, the Sport Director of Bohemians Prague, told me that he thinks a player can be considered "developmental" until between the ages of 21 and 24. His opinion was the most open to players' being late developers of any of the European coaches with whom I talked. Most clubs reserve, or "B," teams were limited to players under 21. So the age of 20 was the cut-off for most of the clubs. It also depends on the structure of the club. Glasgow Celtic and Newcastle United bring in players full time once they are 16. Therefore, Under 16 is a key year for them in evaluating a player.

While it is not fair to keep a player in a club after the club's staff has lost the belief that he can be a professional player, that does not make it easier for the player to accept his dismissal. What is important is that the coach meets with the player to explain why he is not being kept so that he can understand it and, if he is able and motivated, improve himself. In Chapter 4, there are descriptions of the activities clubs undertake to ensure that players have other options. From simple homework support to the schooling provided by English clubs (like Newcastle United) under the FA's Academy Scheme, top European clubs do try to ensure that their players are not solely training for football as boys. Hopefully, the club has helped prepare them for life outside of soccer.

On the bright side, all of the clubs that I visited had little trouble placing their "graduating" players from their oldest youth teams. They were all able to find professional contracts, although perhaps in lower divisions. Munich 1860, above, is one example. All of their Under 18 team players from the 1998-99 season signed contracts with professional clubs for the following season. The other clubs that I visited have similar success placing their graduates.

How Successful Are Professional Clubs at Identifying Youngsters Who Make It as Professionals?

It is difficult to determine how successful specific clubs have been in identifying young talent. From clubs' homepages on the World Wide Web, one can get a sense of how successful they are in signing their own players. Some players they release also end up signing professional contracts elsewhere. Also, if a club signs a player at 16, they may not be doing as much developmental work as his previous club(s). Table 3.1 (page 67) is a very rough estimation of the success rates of the clubs that I visited and some others. I looked at the player profiles on the clubs' World Wide Web pages to see how many first team squad members were graduates of the club's youth program.

In an article from the journal of the English FA Coaches Association, *Insight*, the authors found the following about English clubs signing their youth players to professional contracts: "The figures presented refer only to players who signed as a professional player with the club that they represented as a Youth Trainee [YT] player. A 'success' was defined simply as signing a professional contract. The results do not consider the time that a player remains at a club after signing, or how many games the player actually played for the first team."[31]

From their research, the authors found the following discrepancies between the divisions:

- Top division clubs attract a higher standard of talent due to their status.
- The financial capacity of higher division clubs means that they can "afford" to sign more players on professional contracts, thus offering another year or two to assess potential. Lower-division clubs may only be able to afford to sign players who they "know" will be first team players the following season.
- Squad sizes and squad rotation techniques are greater in the higher divisions. [Clubs playing in the league, the cup, and European

Table 3.1
Sample of Clubs and How Many of Their
Own Youth Players They Have Signed

1999–2000 1st Team Squad members who were in their own clubs' youth system		
Team	*Number*	*Names (age joined if listed)*
Bayern Munich	3	Jarolim (16), Wiblishauser (17), Scheuer (17)
TSV Munich 1860	2	Stranzl, Oller
FC Barcelona	7	Arnau (14), Sergi, Gabri, Guardiola (13), Rosas (13), Xavi (6), Nano (15)
Newcastle United FC	2	Howey, Hughes
Glasgow Celtic FC	2	Burchill, Elliot
Slavia Prague	2	Cerny (6), Petrous (10)
Sparta Prague	8	Postulka (6), Gabriel (12), J. Novotny (14), Jarosik (13), Rosicky (8), V. Svoboda (13), Obajdin (14)
Ajax Amsterdam	5	Knopper, De Cler, Bobson, Pique, O'Brien
Arsenal FC	9	Keown (16), Adams (14), Parlour (15), Pennant (15), Taylor (17), Weston (17), Cole (17), Barrett (16), McGovern (17)
Chelsea FC	2	Clement, Morris
AJ Auxerre	15	Agboh (15), Assati (17), Ciechelski (17), Cisse (14), Cool (14), Danjou (16), Gonzales (14), Jaures (15), Jay (15), Kapo Obou (13), Lecrom (14), Perrier Doumbe (14), Radet (16), Siriex (14), Vandenbossche (14)

Notes: Players are those who are currently in the first team squad and not on loan. To count as "youth" they must join the club before they are 18. Some players join as pros before they are 18 (so they develop elsewhere). Source is team web-page (information is not always included or up to date).

competitions must have enough players to have a fresh team for so many games.]

- Higher division clubs may "cherry pick" the better players from the smaller clubs at an early stage.[32]

Among their conclusions were the following:

• There are limited and reducing opportunities for young players to progress, particularly outside the FA Premier League.
• Although the likelihood of a young player signing a professional contract with an FA Premier League club may be greater than in a lower division club, their rate of progression and first team appearances may be restricted.[33]

While it is not conclusive, this study indicates that the English clubs do sign many of their youth players to professional contracts. My experience at the clubs that I visited suggests that at big European clubs, all of

Table 3.2
Mean Percentage Success Rate of Youth Trainee (YT) Players Signing Professional Contracts with Their Respective English Club for Each Division (for Years 1990/91 to 1995/96)[34]

League	Mean Success Rate
Premier League	53.2 %
Division One	39.9
Division Two	30.7
Division Three	31.4

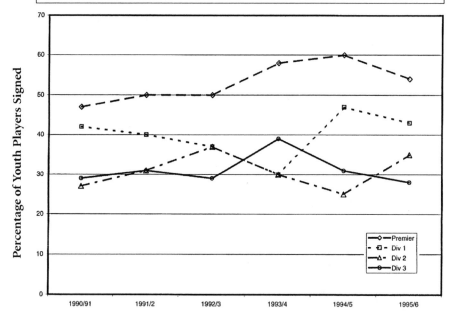

Figure 3.2. Success Rates from Each Division in English Soccer for Each Year Group of YT Players[35]

their oldest players can become professionals at some level. Of the clubs that I visited, Glasgow Celtic, Munich 1860, and Newcastle United had upgraded their youth programs in the last five or six years. The same is true for Bayern Munich.[36] It would be interesting to check back with these clubs in another five to six years to see if they have increased the number of "home-grown" players on their first teams. At that time, the improved youth development programs will have had the time to give their full effect.

Conclusion

Organization is a great aid in being consistent, fair, and accurate in *scouting* players. While big clubs can let players come to them (due to its status in the Czech Republic and its financial limitations, Slavia Prague does), few want to take the chance on missing out on a boy who might turn out to be a superstar. As they are competing for the top talent, most big clubs have a scouting network in place and a system for processing scouting reports.

At the European clubs, tryouts are long, usually a minimum of two weeks of daily training, *after* a player has been scouted in his previous team. Also, because the clubs are in for the long haul with a player, they might not take him right away and continue to observe him to see how he progresses.

Clubs set themselves a difficult task when they choose which young players they want on their teams. They are trying to project into the future five or ten years. There are certain *characteristics* for which they look. Athletic ability and technical ability were the most frequently mentioned traits for which scouts look. Other attributes included attitude (particularly competitiveness and aggression) and awareness (not necessarily tactical expertise, but the ability to see the field). Scientists can help in this process but their work should only be used to include someone who might not have been chosen and never to exclude someone whom the technical staff (coaches and scouts) like. Scientific contributions can only assist soccer experts, they cannot replace them. It is a rare player who will have all of the attributes for which a club is looking. Every coach must prioritize the traits he or she considers most important, which traits can be trained, and which traits cannot be trained. In making these determinations, a knowledge of developmental psychology and physiology is useful. With more longitudinal studies in the years to come, scientists will be able to look at the profiles of successful professionals from when they were children. From such studies, coaches and scouts may be able to use scientific measurements of a player to help determine his potential. Science may come to supplement a coach's or scout's knowledge, but it should never replace it.

Evaluating players in the club is a similar process to scouting players outside the club. Many of the same criteria are in place and the coaches are constantly evaluating the work of their own young players. Most of the clubs that I visited conduct regular evaluations of their players and meet with them to discuss their progress. The clubs also have motivational mechanisms (like pay, provision of training gear, or simply the threat of being dropped) that help them to keep players and to keep players working hard.

While all of the clubs that I visited had to deal with the necessary evil of *releasing players*, they all did it in a dignified way. The coaches met with players and their parents face-to-face. They helped the players find new clubs. As the clubs that I visited were relatively "big clubs," their oldest youth players could count on some kind of professional contract after the end of their youth eligibility (although not necessarily with the club where they were and in clubs as low as the fifth division). In a particularly kind gesture, Glasgow Celtic pays the boy's school fees for one year after he is released.

Due to the difficulty in predicting which boys will turn into professional players, the *success rates* of the clubs in producing players for their first teams will never be 100 percent. With so much money in the game in Europe and the cost of buying a first team player being so high, many clubs have only recently put more emphasis on their youth sectors. It will be interesting to see if the increased interest pays dividends in the next few years.

Once a club has its players, it must work out how much they will train and what the components of training will be. These issues are the topics of the next chapter.

Notes

1. Barend and Van Dorp, p. 220.
2. Cook, Malcolm. *Soccer Coaching and Team Management*. Published by A&C Black, London, 1997, p. 110.
3. *FC Bayern Munich Junior Team*. On Compact Disc. Description of the youth soccer training program at the club with many examples of training exercises.
4. Allen, p. 94.
5. *Ibid.*
6. Barend and Van Dorp, p. 227.

7. Williams et al. "Talent identification in soccer. Sports, Exercise and Injury," in *Insight*. Issue 2, Volume 3, Winter 1999, p. 24.

8. *Ibid.*, p. 25.

9. Williams, Mark, and Tom Reilly. "Talent Identification in Football," in *Insight*. Issue 2, Volume 3, Winter 1999. Published by The Football Association, Potters Bar, Hertfordshire, England, pp. 32–34.

10. Cook, p. 105.

11. Fulham FC web page www.fulhamfc.ac.psiweb.com/football/mn_academy_brochure02.html (17 July 2000).

12. Simmons, Craig. "Strategies for Scouting and Talent Identification of Potential Young Football Players," in *Insight*. Issue 1, Volume 3, Autumn 1999. Published by The Football Association, Potters Bar, Hertfordshire, England, pp. 50–51.

13. *Ibid.*, p. 51.

14. Barend and Van Dorp, pp. 35–36.

15. *Ibid.*, p. 228.

16. Williams, Mark, Tom Reilly, and Andy Franks. "Identifying Talented Football Players: A Scientific Perspective," in *Insight*. Issue 1, Volume 3, Autumn 1999. Published by The Football Association, Potters Bar, Hertfordshire, England, p. 21.

17. Allen, p. 95.

18. *Ibid.*

19. Kormelink and Seeverens, p. 69.

20. *Ibid.*, p. 62.

21. *Ibid.*

22. *Ibid.*, pp. 62–3.

23. *Ibid.*, p. 73.

24. *Ibid.*

25. *FC Bayern Munich Junior Team*. On Compact Disc.

26. Massarella, p. 100.

27. Szymanski and Kuypers, p. 108.

28. Kormelink and Seeverens, p. 73.

29. *Ibid.*, pp. 73–4.

30. Barend and Van Dorp, p. 159.

31. Richardson, Dave, and Rob Cooley. "From Youth Trainee to Professional Contract: An Analysis of Progression," in *Insight*. Issue 1, Volume 3, Autumn 1999. Published by The Football Association, Potters Bar, Hertfordshire, England, p. 34.

32. *Ibid.*

33. *Ibid.*, p. 33.

34. *Ibid.*, p. 34.

35. *Ibid.*

36. *FC Munich Bayern Junior Team*. On Compact Disc.

Chapter 4

Training Timetable
and Components

*The more intensively youth players work, the better they get. We
see it in the so-called small countries all the time. Their players
aren't superhuman; they just work unbelievably hard.*
— Franz Beckenbauer, President,
FC Bayern Munich[1]

*We want school education and football education to go hand in
glove.*
— Tony Carr, Head of Youth Development,
West Ham United[2]

Once a club has organized its youth system, arranged facilities and
equipment, and identified players, it must make decisions about how
much training there will be and what the components of it will be. It must
answer questions such as: How much time do players train? What are the
components of training? How does training change as the players age?
What systems of play will the teams use? What competitions will the teams
enter?

Youth training includes match play because matches are an extension
of training in all of the clubs I visited. As player development, and not
winning, are the first priority, the matches are not an end in themselves.
They are part of the learning process.

This chapter is not about what training exercises the coaches at a club
use. This chapter is about the larger questions of training: how much and
in what areas? There are many training exercises in the Appendices. This
chapter is about how the time is structured: how much do the players play
and what are the different areas in which they train (e.g. tactics and technique)? For these different areas, there are examples of training exercises

in the Appendices. When one understands the areas of training, the exercises are not earth-shaking, although I did see a lot that I have not seen before. My experience is that American coaches use similar training exercises to European coaches. While there were some new exercises, it was more the components of training, not the training exercises, which were different and interesting.

If one had to summarize the training content at clubs in Europe in one word, that word would be "holistic." Modern training involves a holistic approach. Technique and tactics are not enough. All of the clubs which I visited take a great deal of time in other areas of soccer training: coordination, conditioning, nutrition, and psychology. Each club also provided some degree of assistance in personal growth such as support for their academic work, providing academic or vocational training, or employing an education/welfare officer who looked after the players.

FC Barcelona and Glasgow Celtic are the two case studies in this chapter. For the case studies, there is information on the clubs' annual and weekly training schedules. Because the approach to training is holistic, there is an explanation of each club's training in technical, tactical, psychological/ social, and physical realms. The physical training area includes information on coordination and fitness training as well as nutrition. Psychological/social training includes many aspects of creating professionals, teaching youngsters about issues such as responsibility, competing, and working with others. After reviewing the training programs at Barcelona and Celtic, I will describe some unique ideas from other clubs that I visited. They are arranged in alphabetical order. Because there are a lot of different ideas in training, the section of ideas from other clubs is longer than in other chapters. The case studies and other information outline how clubs in Europe have made choices on their soccer "curriculum" regarding how much and what kind of training they will provide. The chapter concludes with a summary of the training process in European clubs.

FC Barcelona: "Running the System"

FC Barcelona is one of the largest and wealthiest football clubs in the world. Many people in their home city and the surrounding region of Catalonia consider "El Barça" to be the Catalan national team. Every day during the season the two sports newspapers in the city carry at least 15 pages of articles about the team. The club runs its own television station to cover the activities of all of the soccer teams and the club's teams in other sports.

With over 100,000 members and a stadium with a capacity of 98,000 spectators, the club is consistently among the elite of Europe.

TRAINING SCHEDULE

The teams at Barça play from August to May. Because the weather is mild through the winter in Barcelona, the teams can train outside throughout the year. The weekly training cycle indicates what they do each week. As one can see from Table 4.1 (page 76), the youth players at Barça play a lot. Training is held so that it does not interfere with school time. Therefore, the players train in the evening on lighted fields. As one can also see in the training schedule, the amount of training per week expands as the players age to where it is similar to the amount of a professional team for the oldest youth players.

Currently, 46 boys live in La Masía, Barcelona's dormitory. The boys living at the residence are mainly from regions of Spain outside of Barcelona but there are also boys from several other countries. They attend schools that are near the club. Boys who do not live in the dormitory live with their families and go to their normal schools. The club holds youth training only in the evening so that it will not interfere with their school time. Only Barça B, Barça C, and the Juvenil A teams train in the mornings. Most of the players on these teams are out of school.

TRAINING COMPONENTS

Every training session that I observed was clearly planned ahead of time and well organized. The thoughtful organization was especially clear in the Football School, where the coaches had clearly organized their sessions together so that they did the same exercises but in different order so that they could use the same prepared areas (like they were moving to different stations). All of the cones were laid out before the players arrived. The coaches walked their teams to and from the locker room. All of the teams had ample equipment: balls, training bibs, cones, flags, hurdles, and goals.

In the words of Llorenc Serra Ferrer, the club's technical director, "there are no tactics without technique." Technical training is therefore a critical part of training at every level. From my observations, the coaches in the club put technical training first.

Since the teams play the same formation (see Figure 4.1) the coaches refer to positions by number and can tell players where to go based on those numbers. It made it possible to organize activities quickly. Perhaps because the teams stick to one system of play, training usually consisted of technique work that often took the form of pattern play based on the team's system. When there was a scrimmage at the end of training, the players were assigned positions that mirrored their positions in a full 11-a-side game.

The club also utilizes nontechnical training. The younger players up to age 14 have special sessions for flexibility, coordination, and agility. The older players also work in these areas and add weight training to their routine.

From my observations, players seem to take a great deal of pride in their training. They take their cleats home every night to polish them. When they are on water breaks, they often stretch or do sit-ups without being asked by the coach (especially the older ones). When the goalkeepers arrive for their special training, they begin warming up on their own. The general skill level of the players was very high. Some players stood out more than others, but there seemed to be no "weak links." The athletic ability of the players was generally impressive.

Many parents did attend training, especially for the younger teams, since they had to transport the children. They watched training quietly from the viewing area. Not once did I hear a parent so much as shout encouragement at the week of training. They let the boys play without interference.

TRAINING EMPHASES AT DIFFERENT AGE GROUPS

Mr. Serra Ferrer did not set specific emphases for the training in each age group. As I wrote above, technical training comes first at every age group. Since the teams all play one of two (similar) systems, the tactical ideas were the same across the different teams. As the players aged, the ideas and exercises were more complex.

SYSTEMS OF PLAY

The Alevines, Infantiles, and Cadetes use the same playing system. Even before Rinus Michels and Johan Cruyff came to the club in the '70s, the younger teams used the 3-4-3 system traditionally used in Holland (see Figure 4.1). The three defenders play zonally. The midfield is arranged in a diamond shape with a stopper, two defensive midfielders, and a playmaker. The forwards include a center forward and two traditional wingers. The reason for this system with the younger players is that the club believes it provides the best opportunities for the players to be creative and express

Table 4.1
Sample Weekly Training Schedule at FC Barcelona

Category	Age	Monday	Tuesday	Wednesday	Thursday	Friday	Saturday	Training Sessions Per Week	Hours Per Week
Barça B	U21	*	10:00 AM, 6:00	10:00 AM	10:00 AM	10:00 AM	Match	5	7.5
Barça C	U21	*	5:30	9:30 AM gym, 5:30	5:30	5:30 AM	Match	5	7.5
Juvenil A	16–18	*	9:30 AM gym, 5:30	5:30	5:00	5:30	Match	6	9
Juvenil B	16–18	*	5:30	6:00	5:30	5:30	Match	4	6
Cadet A	14, 15	6:30	6:30 gym, 7:00	5:30	6:30		Match	4	6
Cadet B	14, 15	6:30	6:30	6:30 gym, 7:00	6:30		Match	4	6
Infantil A	12, 13	7:00	7:00		7:00	7:00	Match	4	6
Infantil B	12, 13	7:00	7:00		7:00	7:00	Match	4	6
Alevin A	10, 11	7:00				7:00	Match	3	4.5
Alevin B	10, 11	7:00		7:00		7:00	Match	3	4.5
Benjamin A + B†	8, 9		7:00		7:00		Match	2	3
Football School‡	6, 7, 8	6:00	6:00	6:00	6:00		Tournament	1	1

Goalkeeper Training (one hour each session)

Juveniles-Cadet A	5:00	Cadet A 5:30	Barça B 5:00	Juvenil A 5:00
Cadet B-Infantiles	6:15	Cadet B 6:15	Barça C 6:00	Juvenil B 7:30
Alevin A	7:00	Infantil A 6:15	Alevin A 6:15	
Alevin B	7:30	Infantil B 7:00	Alevin B 7:00	

Coordination Training:

Barça C and Juvenil A once per week for 1.5 hours.
Cadet A and B 30 minutes per week.

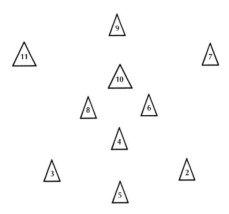

Figure 4.1. System of Younger Youth Teams at FC Barcelona

themselves. The spacing of the players is such that they frequently have the chance to take on defenders 1 v 1 (especially the wingers). From my observations of training, it seemed that the coaches wanted the players to "run the system" as much as to think (collectively) for themselves about how to solve situations in a match. By running the system, the coaches wanted the players to look for certain patterns of play or to prioritize their choices in a certain way. For example, the first option was a long diagonal pass to the winger so he could attack his defender individually.

The older teams all play a 4-3-3 system (see Figure 4.2). The back four play zonally, and they maintain the center forward and two wingers up front. The midfield is arranged with one holding midfielder in the center and two more attacking midfielders on either side of him. (The system is very similar to the one used by the youth teams at FC Bayern Munich.) The first team at Barcelona was using this system when I visited. The attacking play of the youth teams is characterized by all players looking to play forward, especially diagonal balls to the wingers so that they can attack their defenders 1 v 1. For one of the teams, this idea broke

Notes for Table 4.1 (facing page):
All Times are PM unless noted.
Training lasts 1.5 hours unless otherwise noted.
Sundays are free for all players. Sometimes the Juveniles play matches on Sunday.
* Training is only for injured players and those who did not play in the previous match.
† Benjamines train together as one team, then play 7 v 7 matches.
‡ Football School Teams train once per week, so there are three trainings each evening for one hour.
Source: *FC Barcelona*

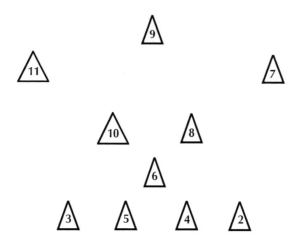

Figure 4.2. System of Juveniles, Barça B, Barça C, and 1st Team

down because the wingers were receiving the ball with their back feet, so that they gave the defenders time to close them down and the wingers ended up facing backward.

It was surprising to see the club play its youth matches on artificial turf, but if anything, it forces the players' technique to be that much tighter. The artificial turf field is also watered down each afternoon so that it is wet when the players are training or playing matches. While I was there the club had just finished the installation of a new artificial turf field with the shaggy "grass" that plays very much like real grass.

COMPETITIONS

All of the teams play in the top league available. From Cadet A down to the Benjamines, they play in leagues based on the city of Barcelona and the surrounding area. The Juveniles play in the "national" league of Catalonia. At the end of each season, the Spanish Football Federation (RFEF) holds tournaments for the winners of the regional championships so that they can crown a Spanish national champion in each of the youth age groups. Barça C plays in Division 4 and Barça B in Division 3 in the national system of Spain. Unlike some clubs, such as Ajax Amsterdam and Bayern Munich, they do not move teams up an age group. They do move players up to an older team if they deem them ready individually. Because the B and C teams are in proper competitions, players from the first team cannot play with them if, for example, they need to work on match fitness after an injury. Also, while the third and fourth divisions do not have any age restrictions, the Barcelona club limits their B and C teams to players under age 21. The teams also play in many tournaments, especially before and after a season.

All of the youth matches I attended were also attended by at least 200 people, with up to 1,000 at the older teams' matches. The usual assortment of parents, siblings, and friends were there. The parents were much more actively rooting for their sons' teams than at training. Many of the spectators were older men, "socios," or members, of the club. These club members/season ticket holders (for the first team) were clearly regulars as they talked about the youth players by first name. The charge to watch the youth teams was 500 pesetas (about $3) but free for the club members. Barça B charged from 1800 to 2700 pesetas ($12 to $18) for their game, which was also broadcast live on local television. Rightly or wrongly, from a very young age Barcelona players must learn to live with all of this scrutiny on their performances.

In the six youth matches I attended, the Barcelona teams won all of them and scored 36 goals with 0 against. Looking at the standings of the leagues in which the various teams compete, the only Barcelona teams that are not in the top three in their respective leagues are the Barça B and C teams which were in the middle of their standings. With so little pressure in most of their games, it must be difficult for the coaches at Barça to maintain desire and concentration in their players, but they took a disciplined approach throughout, even the team that I saw win 16-0. There was no laughing or taunting opponents, selfish play, or even diminished effort when the scores became lopsided.

SUMMARY OF TRAINING AT FC BARCELONA

- Training Schedule: Because the weather is mild in Barcelona throughout the year, the youth teams at Barça are able to train outside all the time. The amount of training per week expands as the players age to where it is similar to the amount of a professional team for the oldest youth players. Their weekly training schedule was typical of most of the clubs that I visited.
- Training Components: Technique is the most important area of training at every age level in the Barcelona youth program. Players also learn to run the Barcelona system which involves moving the ball to the wingers so they can attack. The club does talk with their players about the mentality needed to be a winner. The intense environment also adds to the players' psychological

development. The club undertakes coordination training with its youth players, adding strength training for the older ones.

- Training Emphases at Different Age Levels: There were no set guidelines at different ages, but it was clear that the same messages were sent in increasingly advanced ways. Older and younger teams' training often looked very similar, but the older teams' exercises were a bit more complicated and took place at much higher speed.
- Systems of Play: Barcelona has two set systems of play for their teams that play 11 v 11. The younger teams play 3-4-3. The older teams play 4-3-3. In both cases, they use zonal defending and play with wingers.
- Competitions: Barça's youth teams play in the highest level of competition available to them. Because they have so many talented youngsters, they tend to dominate these competitions. However, they maintain a disciplined approach throughout matches, even lopsided ones.

Glasgow Celtic FC: The Family That Plays Together

Glasgow Celtic Football Club is unique. It has a world-wide following which one could say is truly religious. Indeed, a Catholic priest founded the club, and it has long been known as the Catholic team in Glasgow (city rivals Glasgow Rangers are identified as the Protestant team). In 1967, Celtic became the first British team to win the European Cup. They remain the only Scottish team to do so. They accomplished this feat with a team of players who grew up within an hour's drive of the stadium. Given the club's religious background and the proximity of the players in its best-ever team, one might say Celtic is like a family.

More than any of the six professional soccer clubs where I have had study stays, Celtic has a family atmosphere. Head Youth Coach Willie McStay is a case in point. He and his brother played for Celtic. His son currently plays in the Under 12 team, and his father has been a scout at the club for many years. As will be clear, Celtic goes above and beyond the requirements for running a youth soccer program in Scotland, in large part so that the youth players will have other options if they do not make it as professionals. As Mr. McStay says himself, "Parents are entrusting us with their children, and we need to do more than just teach them to play soccer."

There is a weekly youth training cycle at the club, but it is subject to change. The week I was there, the Under 18 team played a midweek friendly (in part to look at some players on trial in match conditions). Also, because of the Celtic v. Rangers match on Wednesday during the week, youth training was canceled that night.

TRAINING TIMETABLE AND COMPONENTS

The Under 12 through Under 16 teams follow a similar weekly training schedule. The standard time for these teams' training sessions is two hours. On Monday evenings, they report to Celtic Park for coordination and pliometric training. After training, the club provides a healthy dinner for the players followed by homework time for which the club makes tutors available. The club has an Education Coordinator who oversees the club's academic support of its players. The club also provides snacks for the players' parents while they wait for their sons. During these Mondays, the club really builds the "family" atmosphere. They go beyond just soccer training by providing an opportunity for the individual players and for the individual parents to spend time together.

Since fully one-third (or one-fourth for goalkeepers) of the younger players' training time is spent on coordination and pliometric exercises, one must say that there is a strong emphasis on this type of training at the club. Pliometrics are a form of exercise using a lot of jumping to improve a player's muscular power. In the concourse under the stadium where a number of the workouts occurred, the markings for some of the exercises are painted on the floor. One of the sample training sessions in Appendix D is the "fast footwork" routine of the Under 12 team, including some sample exercises from the older teams.

On Tuesdays, the goalkeepers train with the first team's specialist goalkeeping coach. Therefore, the goalkeepers have an extra session each week. During the special session they focus on the technical demands of goalkeeping. The goalkeeping coach is also trying to develop a network of coaches who can work with the 10-year-old "keepers" in Celtic's satellite centers (see below).

On Wednesdays, the younger teams all train, with an emphasis on technical training such as dribbling or passing. After those training sessions, the coaches provide the players with a healthy snack (e.g., juice and fruit).

On Fridays, the teams train with an emphasis on tactical preparation for their up-coming match. They refer to this process as "team shaping." Saturday is free as most of the league matches are on Sundays.

The Under 16 team is in a difficult situation because some of its players are full-time and some are part-time. The part-time players follow the schedule laid out above for the younger teams. The full-time Under 16 players follow the same morning schedule as the Under 18s (see Table 4.2 below) and train on Monday, Wednesday, and Friday evenings with the part-time players on their team.

The program of the Under 18 team is different from that of the younger youth teams because the players are full-time. Every day, the players report at 9 A.M. for breakfast. The club also provides lunch for the players after their morning training session. Mr. McStay said that the club likes providing the meals because it is able to follow the players' diets and ensure that they are eating the right kinds of foods. In Table 4.2, Morning Training usually lasts two hours (from 10:30 to 12:30), although it is usually shorter on Fridays. After the morning training sessions, all of the players have different jobs to maintain the facilities and equipment. The players rotate through the different jobs during a season (e.g., mopping the locker room, taking out the trash, storing equipment). Gym Sessions are in the fitness center in the club's stadium and their primary focus is lifting weights. Because players are often on the Under 18 team for two years, the Sports Psychology classes are divided for the veterans and the new players. On Friday afternoons, the players are responsible for packing hampers with their match uniforms, tracksuits, towels, and whatever other equipment they will need for their game the following day. After the team plays a match on Saturday, some eligible players might go with the Under 16's for their game on Sunday or go with the Under 21's for training on Sunday and a league game on Monday. Other players have Sunday free.

Finally, a number of Celtic's youth players represent their countries (Scotland and Ireland primarily) as youth internationals. Celtic must release players for this duty. The youth coaches do not mind doing it. The travel and experience overseas helps the players' development. Also, as winning is not the primary focus in the youth department, the teams can do without key players. Even if the players are injured while with the youth national teams, Celtic's youth teams can adjust.

TRAINING EMPHASES AT DIFFERENT AGE LEVELS

Mr. McStay and all of the technical staff are currently working hard to discern exactly what path is best for youth training *at Celtic*. Mr. McStay and his coaches are currently wrestling with the dilemma of whether it is better to give coaches a lot of guidelines or to allow them the space to use their own ideas. Currently, training emphases at various ages include:

Table 4.2
Under 18 Weekly Training Program

Day	Morning Training Focus	Afternoon		
Mon.	General/Skills	1:30 Skills Specific/Spring Coaching	3:00 Sports Physiology (1st Year)	4:00 Diet/Nutrition Sports Science
Tues.	Physical/ Technical	1:30 Gym Session	3:00 Sports Psychology (2nd Year)	
Wed.	College/SVQ*	College/SVQ		
Thur.	General Session (Functional)	1:30 Gym Session	2:30 Sprint Coaching	
Fri.	Pre-match session (Team Play)	Prepare Uniforms and Equipment for Match		
Sat.	Match Day	Watch 1st Team Match		
Sun.	Rest OR Some prepare for U-21 or U-16 matches			

*SVQ is the "Modern Apprenticeship": The club provides
vocational training in recreation facility management.
Source: Celtic Football Club

- *12/13-year-olds*: Technical work, especially being able to play with both feet. They also want players to be able to solve small group situations such as 1 v 1, 2 v 2, and 4 v 4. They want the players to start learning about basic team shape.
- *14/15-year-olds*: Start to focus on more thorough match preparation such as 7 v 6 situations on goal and movement in relation to one another. They start to make the transition from individual to team players.
- *16-year-olds*: Start to mix in with the professional players. They learn about being "winners" and having a strong mentality.
- *17-year-olds and older*: develop an "edge" in their attitudes and start to prepare to play with the first team.

He added that from 16 years old, the players have more comprehensive training in two senses. They start to work directly with the coaches in tangential areas, such as fitness or psychology. They also have more detail in their work: from small-sided games to simulated pressure in their technical work, to shadow defending in 7 v 6 situations.

There are several references in the list of training emphases above to the players' psychological development. Scottish players are traditionally very competitive. Furthermore, within Scotland, second best is not good enough for Celtic and its supporters. The club's role as one of the two elite clubs in the country and their rivalry with Rangers breeds a strong will to win. Because of the history and the environment, the club does not spend time specifically trying to cultivate competitiveness in its players. Mr. McStay believes that culture and environment "train" the players' mental toughness and will to win.

Systems of Play

During the 1999-2000 season, Celtic had a new general manager. One of Mr. McStay's first questions for him pertained to what system the youth teams should play. The general manager replied that he was not worried about what system the youth teams played. He wanted them to play different systems and focus on learning the principles of play, rather than systems. Therefore, individual team coaches were free to choose the formation in which their team would play. While not uncommon, this idea stands in Celtic in contrast to clubs like Ajax, Barcelona, and Bayern where the club dictates a certain system for the youth teams.

Competitions

As mentioned above, the leagues run by the Scottish Premier League and the Scottish Football League cover the whole of Scotland. The season runs from the end of August to the beginning of May. Celtic's Under 18 team has won its league three of the last five years. The Under 18 league plays with standard rules: 45 minute halves, three substitutions without reentry.

There are some special rules in the leagues for the Under 16 and younger teams to ensure the focus is on player development. They do not keep standings. They play three or four periods (usually four if there is a strong wind and they want to even out any advantage from it). There is open substitution; the coaches can send players in and out of matches. Most of the Celtic coaches allocate periods to their players, rather than run them in and out during play. Martin Miller, the Under 13 coach, has an interesting approach to preparing his players for their match play. On Friday after training, he hangs posters on the wall of the locker room. The posters include the line-ups for each period and the players' roles on different set plays. The players are then responsible to move around the room to write down the information that pertains to them for the game.

The Scottish Football Association (SFA) also runs a Youth Cup competition for Under 18 teams. The Cup is a knockout competition. After one loss, a team is out of the competition. The matches for the Youth Cup occur in the stadiums of clubs' first teams. The benefit for developing professionals is that they gain familiarity with playing in literal and figurative "big arenas." Celtic's Under 18 team has won the SFA Youth Cup three of the last four years.

SUMMARY OF TRAINING AT GLASGOW CELTIC

- Training Timetable: Even with the unpredictable weather in Glasgow, Celtic's teams train outside all year round. The players are not bothered by cold, windy, or rainy conditions. There is a short break in the season during January. For the older players, there is not as much training each week as at clubs in other countries.
- Training Components: Physical training at Celtic is very advanced. One night each week is totally given over to coordination training. The club has a nutritionist, a physiologist, and a fitness coach. Celtic provides meals for their players so it can monitor and teach nutrition. The club relies on the natural trait of British/Scottish players to be good competitors, but it also is active in honing their "edge." To help with psychological training, the club has a full-time sports psychologist. Technical and Tactical training are nominally the topics of certain training sessions. The club tries to leave no stone unturned in training their youth players.
- Training Emphases at Different Age Levels: Celtic's coaches are constantly working to decide on the best path for Celtic's youth players; what the key elements of training are at different ages. At this time, Celtic follows the trend of most clubs, in that the emphasis for the youngest players is totally on technique and tactics become a bigger and bigger part of training as the players age.
- Systems of Play: While the teams tended to play 4-4-2, there was some variation. Each coach is free to decide on his own, there is no guideline from the club.
- Competitions: The Celtic youth teams play in the top competitions available to them and do very well. Often, their best competition comes in training.

Ideas from Other Clubs

TSV MUNICH 1860

The most impressive part of 1860's youth set up was the clear thought they have put into the components of their youth training and the emphases at different ages. For example, they know that they must keep the game fun to keep their players interested and enthusiastic. The School Pilot Project (see Chapter 2) contains a small-sided-games component so the players can simply enjoy playing. The players in the club are encouraged, and even taken by their own coaches, to play other sports. The Under 16 coach, Ernst Thaler, told me how he takes his team regularly for in-line hockey, basketball, and other sports so that they can regenerate after a match, enjoy some time together as a team, and just have fun. The week after I visited Munich, Mr. Tanner, the head of the youth sector, was accompanying one of the youth teams for a week of skiing in Austria (paid for by one of 1860's supporters' clubs!). As Mr. Tanner summarized, the club likes to use other sports for variety and also to help boys improve their over-all coordination.

Another area into which the club has put a lot of thought is how to provide developmentally appropriate soccer activities for their players. For example, the youth teams play many different systems of play. Rather than leaving it up to the individual coach, 1860 has a preferred system for each age group. Each one provides the players opportunities to learn certain aspects of the game better than others. Mr. Tanner said that the club believes that players must learn, above all else, to win 1 v 1 duels, both offensively and defensively. Once they have mastered this skill, they can and should learn zonal defending. From the age of 13, they want the players to learn zonal defending with a lot double-teaming. They must learn to attack in a zone by watching players and not mark space. He added that the use of wingers gives those players a chance to develop as dribblers, to specialize in that aspect of 1 v 1 play. Systems of Play are a big difference between Bayern and 1860. As explained above, Bayern has one system for all of its youth teams. 1860 has different systems that emphasize certain activities (e.g. 1 v 1 duels, zonal defending) so that the players will gain experience in them.

Mr. Tanner shared another interesting tactical idea. His preference is that the players only use long passes across the field as a last resort. It is difficult to be accurate with long passes and they are difficult to control. By trying to play shorter passes, there is better likelihood that they will be accurately played and properly controlled.

From the Under 13 team and older, the players begin fitness testing. The coaches use the tests to see what kind of special training the team and or individuals might need. The players do an anaerobic endurance test in which blood lactate is measured twice each year, in July (during preseason), and February (at the end of the winter break). The test involves four 1600-meter runs on a track at progressively higher speeds: 3 km/h, 3.5 km/h, 4 km/h, and 4.5 km/h. The players hear a beep from a tape at certain intervals and that sets the pace for them. Blood samples are taken before and after each run.

For players who need extra work on their endurance, 1860 has a course in the woods near its training facility. There are signs along the path every 200 meters. The player runs with a walkman that is playing a tape with beeps at certain intervals. The player must reach each sign at the beep.

The club does not closely monitor the players' diets. I did ask Mr. Tanner about dietary supplements. It surprised me to learn that the club had used the dietary supplement Creatine with players as young as 13 years old. Mr. Tanner explained that they used it with the young players for a short period when they had a very heavy schedule. He added that no player should use Creatine supplements regularly, as one's body will demand more and more yet produce less and less of its own. He said he had heard of clubs where the (professional) players were taking so much Creatine every day that they must have been eating the pills "with a spoon."

Watching the matches was also interesting. The referee is able to give a player a five-minute "penalty" or cooling off period during which he must go to the sideline, and his team plays short-handed. He can return to the game after five minutes elapses. The five minutes can be given to a player before, after, or with a yellow card. The coaches with whom I spoke said that the five-minute penalty was supposed to come between the yellow and red card as an intermediate step. The teams from Under 11 and older all play with standard rules of no reentry and two halves. The two halves are progressively longer as the players age.

I found the behavior of the coaches at the matches interesting. During the games of two different teams, one coach was stationed on each sideline. While the coaches can communicate more easily with all of the players during the match, the players are then receiving a lot of instructions from their coaches, instead of making their own decisions.

Newcastle United FC

The FA largely dictates the weekly training cycle. As shown in Table 2.1 in Chapter 2, the teams train according to FA guidelines. The boys

Table 4.3
Under 17/Under 19 Weekly Training Cycle

DAY	A.M.	P.M.
Monday	College	Training, followed by Conditioning/ Coordination Training
Tuesday	Training*	Training*
Wednesday	Training*	Conditioning/ Coordination Training
Thursday	College	College
Friday	Training	
Saturday	Match	
Sunday	Free	Free

*Goalkeepers with goalkeeper coach.

in the Under 17 and 19 teams train more often than the younger teams because they are full time in the Academy (see Table 4.3 above). Training, especially for the older teams, typically runs two hours.

Regarding training emphasis, Assistant Academy Director Vince Hutton added that Academy Director Alan Irvine has a preference that the emphasis in training should be on passing. All aspects of passing are important: the quality of the pass, the first touch, the body shape on reception (sideways on), and the look away by the receiver as the ball is traveling to him so he can be aware of the situation around him. He also said that, for the younger players, ball manipulation is critical.

In Mr. Irvine's words, "I know how to make the players tired, but not necessarily how to make them fit." He is glad that the club retains the conditioning coaches because it helps to ensure that the players are fit in the ways they should be. The Under 17 and 19 players had specific conditioning/coordination training two times each week. Mr. Hutton has worked out an interesting plan for the younger teams. The fitness coach rotates through the six younger teams, working with one each week. During the intervening weeks, the team coaches continue with the exercises (usually just two at a time) that the conditioning coach has shown them. The hope is that the coach of each age group team will develop a repertoire of exercises for his specific age group. Since the coaches stay with the same age group from year to year, they can become experts on the conditioning and coordination skills for their age group.

Through a research project on injuries that the club is carrying out under direction from the FA, they have decided that flexibility is the only conditioning focus for the Under 14 players. They believe that this makes sense since boys in that age group are often growing so fast that they are very susceptible to certain types of injuries (e.g. hamstring pulls).

Finally, the club maintains a logbook for each player in which the coaches keep track of progress and activity. The coaches can use the logs to keep close track of how much time a player has put in, as well as to make observations about players' improvements.

Unlike many countries where a handful of clubs dominate and have all of the best youth players (and professional ones too), there are many clubs in England where the opportunity exists to find roughly equivalent training opportunities. The FA Academy leagues are competitive in the sense that no single club dominates them. It means that clubs do not have to worry about playing their teams in older age groups to find competition for them. At the older age groups, Newcastle does move individual players up, if they feel that they are ready.

Newcastle United also participates in the FA Youth Cup. Similar to the Scottish Youth Cup, it is a knockout competition for Under 18 teams. The matches are played in clubs' stadiums with all the ceremony of first team league or cup matches. The two quarterfinals I watched were attended by approximately 7,000 people each.

Mr. Irvine and the Newcastle coaches take different views of the FA Youth Cup and their league competition. They consider the league games to be an extension of training. They do not worry about results or preparing for specific opponents. On the other hand, for the FA Youth Cup, with its surrounding hoopla, they try much harder to win. They see it as a chance to teach the boys about not only playing well but also playing well in the spotlight. For many of the players, it is their first experience with large stadiums and crowds of more than parents and friends watching the match. It is an opportunity to prepare them for being a professional player in every sense. Even in the Cup, the coaches keep their perspective. They were very pleased that they had a draw in an early round with local rival Sunderland, as it meant there would be a replay and an extra opportunity for the players to play in a big stadium.

SK SLAVIA PRAGUE

In contrast to most of the other clubs which I visited, coaches at Slavia Prague have a lot of freedom to work according to their own experience and beliefs. This means they introduce tactical and physical training as they see fit. It is difficult, therefore, for Mr. Prochazka, the youth chief, to enforce training emphases for different age groups. He has disagreements with a number of coaches who do nothing but shooting and play scrimmages with half of the team playing against the other half. Especially at the younger age groups he finds this unacceptable. For the training of the youngest players, as he put it, "the game has requirements." They must play in small-sided games: 1 v 1, 2 v 2, and 3 v 3. The boys must develop quick feet and learn to control their bodies. The majority of their training must be with the ball. In fact, he believes that the emphasis with young players should be on dribbling. It is his belief that dribblers can learn to pass later but that passers cannot learn to dribble at an older age.

Mr. Prochazka added that Czech players often have a problem with the competitive mentality. Because Slavia is one of the biggest clubs in the country, players can be complacent once they enter the club. The coaches at Slavia must constantly grow the players' interest and motivate them all the time. The coaches in the club also use a lot of races or training games, after which the losing team must do sit-ups or some other exercise.

Because the league divides its season into two halves with a three-month break in the middle, the coaches at Slavia have a lengthy training period with very few matches. During the winter break, the coaches sometimes take their players to play other sports such as basketball, team handball, gymnastics, or swimming. The idea is that the players will find it enjoyable so they can maintain their enthusiasm. Also, activities such as gymnastics and tumbling help their coordination.

Most of the Slavia youth teams play a 3-5-2 system that one could describe as typically Czech. There is a sweeper and the team man-marks their opponents. Mr. Prochazka coaches one of the teams and it plays a zonal back four. Again, it is up to the individual coach.

Because so much of what the Slavia youth system does is up to the individual coach, the club must try to find the best coaches it can. We will investigate how well they, and other clubs, do in terms of coaching in the next chapter.

Summary

From the information given above about the many clubs that I visited and researched, one can see there are many interesting ideas in the areas of training timetables and components. Some of the ideas conflict. For example, should a club's youth teams all play the same system? There are certainly valid arguments for different sides of the question. What is important is that those running youth soccer clubs and teams think about the timetables and components of training so that there is a coherent development plan. Players will develop best if they follow a systematic plan of development rather than going in a different direction every year. The sections below contain key ideas for training timetables, training components, training emphases at different age levels, systems of play, and competitions.

TRAINING TIMETABLE

Youth players in top Europeans clubs play a lot. The season is long and the players train several times every week. The players also spend time together with their teammates whether they attend school together, eat meals together, or do homework together. If the players want to pursue a professional career, it stands to reason that the more they play, the more they will improve. People marvel at concert pianists who trained three hours per day as children. It is okay for youth soccer players to train a lot, as long as other areas of their development are not neglected.

An interesting idea for a club's annual training program comes from DVS '33, a small club in Holland. They have a detailed annual plan for their youth players' training. Each age group has its own annual program, which is broken down into four ten week periods. Each annual program contains precise details of the coaching priorities.[3] While DVS '33 is not a household name, even in Holland, their idea is an interesting one. Youngsters develop at different rates and so a season-long planned training program could have to be changed. However, if the emphasis is on learning the game and not on winning, players must be introduced to all of the facets of the game. If math teachers can plan a year's algebra curriculum, coaches can plan a year's soccer curriculum, as long as they are willing to be flexible.

TRAINING COMPONENTS

At the end of October 1999, the European Union of Football Trainers met for their annual conference. The topic of the conference was "The Development of European Talent." The coaches from across Europe agreed on the following points:

- Development should be fun for the children above all other considerations.
- Coaches working with young children should concentrate on developing those skills necessary for players to cope with all the demands of 1 v 1.

- In line with the above, the Conference felt that current trends placed too much emphasis on passing and the sense of order that comes with it.
- Again there was unanimous agreement that "time" spent with the ball is the key.
- Sensitive boarding for elite youngsters was something which the coaches saw as an increasing possibility and need, in order to really attack the "time" question.[4]

The clubs I visited were all active in some way in developing the psychological/social side of their players. Part of this was motivated by their own self-interest. They want to develop professional players in every way. Therefore, youth players must learn responsibility, communication, dealing with pressure, and other traits. Some of the clubs appeared to have a genuine sense of obligation to help their youth players develop as people. Others were willing to help with academics only so the player would be able to concentrate on playing, i.e., more of a selfish motive. Clubs also took into account the traditional cultural norms in which their players grow up. For example, the British clubs felt that they did not need to worry about developing their players' competitive spirits since British players are traditionally endowed with determination. At the same time, courage, aggressiveness, and positive attitude were traits that several clubs mentioned as ones they look for in players they are scouting. Glasgow Celtic was the only club that I encountered which had a full-time club sports psychologist. It was a sign, I believe, of how important Celtic considers psychological development of their players.

There are many areas of physical development. Nutrition, coordination (agility, balance, flexibility, and coordination), quickness, strength, speed, and fitness are just some of them. Each of the clubs that I visited put a lot of thought into age-appropriate physical development activities. Some clubs (Newcastle, Celtic) even provided meals for their players. The clubs generally agreed that physical training was not as important as technical and tactical training. However, some noted that it was difficult for older youth players to join their club, in large part because they were not as fit and coordinated as the players already in the club.

It appears that specific fitness training is not important for youth players. Danish soccer fitness expert Jens Bangsbo cited a Danish study in which "boys younger than 15 years had a pronounced increase in performance on a fitness test with age, despite not doing specific fitness training. Furthermore, the results of the 18-year-old players were as high as those of the senior league players. It appears that a player can reach a top-class level as a senior player without performing fitness training during the younger years." Bangsbo added, "The time saved by excluding fitness training should be spent on training to improve technical skills, as the players will greatly benefit from this type of training when they become seniors."[5]

On the UEFA "A" license course, professors from Charles University presented physical training ideas from gymnastics, track, and swimming. The track coach provided lessons in proper running technique and fast starts. He introduced a number of running drills done over 20 meters. Running technique is important both to conserve energy and to run faster.

The swimming coach demonstrated a number of flexibility and strengthening exercises using the water as resistance. If a player runs in the water, for example, it provides low level resistance for strengthening purposes and almost zero pounding for the body. It is particularly useful for regeneration after a match or rehabilitation after an injury.

The gymnastics coach, Dr. Miroslav Zitko, presented a number of interesting ideas. Because there are no soccer balls or teammates, gymnastics provides many straightforward ways of training flexibility, agility, balance, coordination, and strength. A number of the clubs that I visited sent their players for gymnastics as part of their physical training. Dr. Zitko had devised a number of flexibility and strength tests. One example of a flexibility test is for the player to stand with his legs shoulder width apart and interlace his fingers behind his back. He should bend at the waist, keeping his back straight, as far forward as possible. At the same time, he should pull his arms as far away from his body as he can. The player should be able to bend at the waist more than 90 degrees and pull his arms away from his back more than 30 degrees. There are many other interesting ideas in Dr. Zitko's book (see the Bibliography).

I also saw him work with a 16-year-old goalkeeper. He put the goalkeeper through a one-hour workout which provided a number of activities for the "keeper" to work on his strength and coordination. In every case, the player's body weight was the only resistance. For example, the player had to dive over a swing, doing a somersault. After the somersault, he rolled sideways, and then had to get up to dive over the swing again before it swung back over him. A goalkeeper able to complete a workout full of difficult gymnastics activities would have little trouble with the physical demands of being a goalkeeper. Most clubs that I visited employed a full-time fitness expert who could bring in physical training ideas from other athletic disciplines.

One of my favorite lines from a coach came from Mr. Serra Ferrer at Barcelona. It bears repeating: "*There are no tactics without technique.*" Even players with terrific vision, awareness, and insight cannot act on their ideas unless they have the technique to carry out their plans.

I saw very little of what I would call strictly tactical training. Most of it seemed to take place on the blackboard before a match. At Barcelona, there was a lot of pattern play in training so that coaches were showing players which decisions to make. The coaches showed the players certain patterns in which to run and pass similar to a basketball play. Newcastle and Celtic had the most specific "team-shaping" exercises.

TRAINING EMPHASES AT DIFFERENT AGES

From the hundreds of hours of youth training that I observed at clubs in Europe, technical training received great emphasis in every age group including professional teams. In fact, I was surprised that there was so little tactical training, at every level. There is some debate on whether the initial focus of technical training should be on passing or dribbling. The report from the European Union of Football Trainers indicates their preference for dribbling. It was interesting to see the Under 10 teams of Munich 1860 and Slavia Prague. The Slavia players were indeed focused on dribbling. All of their players were eager to take on a player when they were in possession of the ball. Their combination play was sporadic. 1860's youngsters played a number of beautiful combinations but were not as eager to attack 1 v 1.

Munich 1860 has the very good conception of tactical development: Players must first learn to battle in 1 v 1 confrontations, both on offense and defense. Therefore, players must spend time playing in systems that utilize man-marking and wingers (since they have a lot of opportunities to attack defenders 1 v 1). They should also learn to play with zonal defending. Zonal defending is better than man marking for teaching principles of defending. The systems of play and training emphases of their youth teams reflect these ideas. Also, given the frequency with which professional teams change their coaches, players must be able to adapt to different tactical demands and the different positions that different systems of play require. What is important is that they learn principles of play, not a system of play.

SYSTEMS OF PLAY

The system, or formation, that a team uses is not as important as the players' understanding of the game. The system can be a powerful teaching tool of the principles of play and so it is an important consideration in the training of youth players. Barcelona, Ajax, and Bayern Munich have a set system of play, or team formation, for their youth teams. There are advantages to this idea. It makes training easy to organize. The players have a clear conception of their roles. *If*, and it is a big if since first team coaches change so often, the first team is playing the same system, young players will be able to step smoothly into a role with the first team. Mr. Serra Ferrer at Barcelona said that the systems the Barça teams use are most conducive to providing players the chance to take on defenders 1 v 1. The disadvantages of being tied into one system are that it is predictable for opponents; you must find players who can handle the tactical demands of the system; and if players leave that club, they may have a difficult time adjusting to playing in another system. Within two years of winning the European Cup in 1995, most of Ajax's players moved to new clubs. Many of them had trouble at their new clubs. Interestingly, when the coach of that Ajax team, Louis Van Gaal, moved to Barcelona, he brought in many of the players from that team so that he could implement what he calls "his system."

Other clubs, such as Newcastle and Glasgow Celtic, do not focus on the system their youth teams play. They want the players to be able to adapt to a number of systems.

As described above, Munich 1860 intentionally uses specific systems at different ages so that certain aspects of the game will be emphasized. This is an interesting idea. The players have the benefit of learning to be flexible and also the benefit of playing in certain positions that allow them to focus on certain elements of the game. For example it is different for a player to be right wing in a 3-forward formation than to be the right midfielder in a 4-player midfield with 2 forwards. Combining the two advantages, as 1860 does, is an excellent idea. 1860 receives the advantages of their players learning to play in different systems and the teaching advantages of different systems. For youth teams, systems are an important teaching tool for the principles of play and 1860 considers the message that they send carefully.

COMPETITIONS

The area covered by youth leagues expands as the players age. For younger teams, up to Under 15 or 16, some countries modify the rules to allow reentry and multiple periods of play. They have these changes so that the coaches can have more contact with players during a match for educational purposes. Interestingly, the coaches whom I observed in the countries with these rules did not shout as much to their players during the course of play. As the coach must use the match as a learning experience, he should talk with the players, but he should not run the match for them. The rule changes seemed to help the coach find the right balance between helping the players and letting them play. In most countries (Spain was the big exception) rules for the older players were the same as for professionals: no reentry and three substitutions from five reserves.

The emphasis in each country was on league play. Teams did play in tournaments, but these tournaments were only to keep in shape during the winter, prepare for the season, or finish the season. England and Scotland hold national youth cup competitions in addition to the leagues.

European clubs spend a lot of time and effort on youth training. Because they have the time and resources, the youth training is holistic and detailed. The ideas in this chapter are only a small sample of the training ideas of European clubs. I have included them here to give a flavor of the different possibilities. There are a lot of good ideas in youth development in Europe. There are so many that clubs must prioritize what is important, especially since some of the ideas contradict one another. What is important is to think about different ideas in training and coaching and decide for yourself which you will use.

Once a club has organized teams, arranged for facilities and equipment, located players, identified and prioritized the components of training, and set a training schedule, it is up to the coaches to put all of these ingredients together to develop players. In Chapter 5, we will look closely at the coaches in the European clubs: their experience, their training, and their behavior.

Notes

1. *FC Bayern Munich Junior Team.* On Compact Disc.
2. Allen, p. 95.
3. Kormelink and Seeverens, pp. 5–6.
4. Wilkinson, Howard. "Message from Howard Wilkinson," in *Insight.* Issue 1, Volume 3, Autumn 1999. Published by The Football Association, Potters Bar, Hertfordshire, England. Inside cover.
5. Bangsbo, Jens. *Fitness Training in Football: A Scientific Approach.* HO + Storm, Bagsvaerd, Denmark. 1994, pp. 110–111.

Chapter 5

Coaches

You can learn a brilliant book full of coaching drills by heart, but the ability to act at the right moment, to make an accurate analysis and to show how things should be done, is much more important. That is the heart of the matter!
— Co Adriaanse, Former Director of Youth
Development at Ajax Amsterdam[1]

In an age where many children have more sedentary options than going out to play, they are unlikely to be active outdoors unless they are in an organized setting. An organized setting implies that there must be adult involvement. If there are going to be adults involved, they must provide an experience for the kids that is fun and stimulating. In soccer it means there must be a coach. A good coach. Defining a good coach is difficult. Because players have varied ages, personalities, and needs, good coaches come in many different types. At the end of this chapter, after looking at the literature and reviewing the club visits, I will attempt to define a "good coach."

Chapters 2 through 4 reviewed the organization, facilities, equipment, environment, player evaluation, and training activities of European soccer clubs. Coaches are responsible for combining all of these elements to create top-class players. They must use the tools at their disposal to help the players improve and become both better people and better players.

Each of the clubs that I visited chose as carefully as possible the right people to coach in their youth programs. Information from my research of literature and my coaching course in the Czech Republic sheds light on a number of key issues for coaches. The key issues relate to coaches' roles in training exercises and their interaction with players. First, I will review some important ideas about coaching so that one can bear them in mind when reading about the clubs. For this chapter, I have chosen to use Newcastle United and FC Barcelona as case studies. The styles of the two groups of coaches were very different. The coaches at Newcastle were informal, but not casual. The coaches at Barcelona were formal and often very intense. The activities that the coaches arranged in training contrasted also. The coaches at Newcastle tended to use more "free play" and teach within it. At Barcelona, there was a lot of pattern play in training. After the case studies, there is a conclusion of the chapter. Ideas on coaching from other clubs or the literature are in the conclusion or else I have incorporated them into other chapters of the book.

Two Key Issues in Coaching: Organizing and Teaching

There are two ways coaches can affect players' learning. The first is the type of training exercise. The coach must be an organizer. If the coach can create a learning atmosphere simply by how he organizes training, he will have been very successful. For example, many European soccer coaches talk about re-creating "street soccer." The idea here is to put the players in an environment similar to the one in which kids used to play in the streets. In any case, the medium is the message. If players do nothing but technique drills in training, they will not be able to make decisions in games of when to use certain techniques. The game is a terrific teacher on its own.

The second way coaches can affect the learning of their players is the type of coaching in which they engage during training. The coach must also be a teacher. It is not enough to be an organizer. How does the coach act within a training exercise? What is his teaching style? Sometimes players need to "discover" how to do something through trial-and-error, other times they need exact instructions. Teaching style depends on the topic, the players, and the ways in which a coach is comfortable working. For example, when I play soccer with my four-year-old son and his friends, there is very little verbal instruction. They each have a ball and we play "Follow the Leader," "Copy Cat," or we have races.

These are difficult questions. A good coach will be able to recognize that different types of training activities are best at different times. Similarly, a coach must use different techniques of teaching. He must consider how he works best, how the team learns best, how individual players learn best, how a topic is best taught. These considerations are also affected by the mental state of the team, the timing of the training before a match, and the skill or tactic that the coach wants to train. To consider all of these factors, planning is important but a coach must be flexible if, for example, the players' mood is not what he thought it would be on a certain day.

ORGANIZATION OF TRAINING

In the United States, we break down technical training into three areas: basic, match-related, and match conditions activities. Technical training is training in which the objective is to help a player improve his ability with the ball, not only to control it, but be able to do it under pressure. We divide tactical training into games with no goals, one goal, and then two goals (alternatively, some think of it as no goals, small goals, big goals). Tactical training means training players how to make the right decisions in a game. In Czech coaching courses, the instructors break down all training into three areas: technical exercises (in which there are no variables of time, space, or defender), game exercises (which involve players using their perceptions to make decisions, but there is a certain stop and start), and training games (continuous, but they have learning conditions imposed, e.g. a team must attack using the flank zone). Regardless of which system one uses, in each case the similarity to a real game increases with each stage. The more variability there is in an activity, the more the exercise is similar to regular soccer.

A different, more detailed, method for dividing training activities (with brief descriptions) from the work of English coach Malcolm Cook is:

- Freeze Play: the coach stops the players while they are playing to review a situation or to give them a picture of it.
- Drillwork: the players have a lot of repetitions without a lot of pressure. Useful as a warm-up.
- Conditioned Play: The coach makes a special rule or scoring system that causes the players to emphasize a certain aspect of play (e.g., players are limited to two touches).
- Repetitive Pressure Play: Similar to drillwork except that one player works continuously (e.g., a coach shoots balls at a goalkeeper while being fed balls by a server so that one shot follows another rapidly).

- Shadow Play: A group or team plays against imaginary or heavily outnumbered opposition, to focus on patterns and timing of play.
- Functional Play: A player or players work in the area of their normal area of the field on an aspect of the game which they commonly do (e.g., flank players receive the ball near the touchline and cross it into the penalty area).
- Phase Play: Similar to functional play, although with more players. Groups of players operate in a key area of the field for them (e.g., the midfielders play in the middle third of the field).
- Coaching in the Game: While the players are playing a regular game, the coach comments on their performance. The coach can implement freeze play into this activity.[2]

Regardless of how one breaks down the different types of training, it is important to understand that there are different ways for a coach to put his message across based on how he organizes training. Some methods are more effective than others for certain coaches and for certain topics in the game. The coach must choose the method that will be most effective for teaching his players.

All players, from the three-year-old beginner to the 30-year-old world-class star, need technical training. For example, youngsters need to learn to control the ball under pressure of a defender. Professionals do not need to learn to control the ball under pressure, but they do need to practice it so they will be sharp in a match. Players need to learn new techniques, to master techniques they know, or to keep techniques they have mastered working well. They also need to simply play soccer in training. It maintains the fun for the players and is the most realistic training they can do. From my observations in Europe, coaches at every level undertake these activities. The key question, for me, is *what happens in between the basic technical work and the scrimmage at the end of training?* That is the area in which the coach must do his teaching. The coach must create activities in which the players are forced to learn: to tighten their technique, to turn technique into skill by deciding when to use it, and to make good decisions. These are questions that were presented in Chapter 4. Of course, the coach must be active during these activities, not just arrange them.

Behavior Within Training

The second way coaches can decide on how they will affect players is how they interact with players in the activities they organize. In education, it is called "teaching style." Different activities are conducive to different styles of teaching. For example, during a shooting drill in which the players are having many repetitions, the coach can pull a player aside to talk and work with him individually. During a 5-a-side game, it is difficult for a coach to do this since the player's team will be at a serious disadvantage without him. To make a coaching point, the coach will have to stop the game and show everyone what he wants them to see. Another example: at Glasgow Celtic, the Under 18 team was playing eight attackers against seven defenders. When the attackers had the ball, the coach would occasionally stop the play and elicit ideas from the players as to how they could solve the attacking situation. It was different from Barcelona, where in a similar situation, the coach would have provided the players with the "correct" attacking move. Whatever the method, the teaching part of coaching is about changing players's behaviors.

Former director of the Ajax youth sector, Co Adriaanse: "Obviously the ability to explain things in terms that young children can understand is a gift. This is why Ajax has made a conscious decision to use a young coach with teaching abilities to coach the youngest players. He has to be young because the age gap should never be too wide."[3] Mr. Adriaanse's hope is that young coaches will be able to relate better to their players. The relationship of the coach and player are important if the coach is going to affect the player's behavior.

If he does nothing more than organize training, the coach is not maximizing the learning opportunities for his players. According to a recent study,[4] players who received feedback from their coaches, either with words or video tape, improved more than players who did not receive feedback.

Of course, coaches have different personalities. It is important that the coach be himself but also be able to interact in a number of ways with his players. For example, I once observed a coach at a military school who, while appearing to be a "military" man, was very relaxed with his players. His belief was that the players had enough discipline and structure in their lives and that he did not need to add to it. In my opinion, he was an excellent coach in that he taught his players how to play, without being a drill sergeant. Another example: I will never forget a training session in college where my coach went into a profanity-laced tirade against our team's captain. While the coach was a little mad at the player, he was really mad that the whole team was not working as hard as he wanted. By yelling at the captain, who we all knew was the hardest worker on the team, he gave the rest of us the message. Also, the coach knew that the captain had the personality to accept such a verbal barrage. While the coach's method is not my favorite, the coach was able to get his message across, even to those with fragile self-esteem, using his knowledge of what form of communication he thought would work best in that situation.

Hopefully, a coach will take into account the needs of his players to use the style that they need. The crucial question is: "What teaching method will a coach use?" After organizing the activity (which sends a message to the players), the coach must decide the questions he will ask (e.g., How does one shoot accurately?), and finally the correct answers (e.g., the planted foot should point at the target). The other issue for the coach is how much he or she will provide direction, questions, and answers and how much the players will determine them. There are many ways to delineate coaching styles. One, from the work of educators Muska Mosston and Sara Ashworth, identifies the following teaching/coaching styles (with brief descriptions):

- Dominant Style: The coach does everything — organizes the exercise, demonstrates how to do it, and how to do it correctly. Useful for introducing a new skill or exercise (technique drills in which the players have many repetitions).
- Practice Style: The coach still does all organizing and poses the questions, but the students make many decisions themselves. The coach moves around giving advice to the players.
- Reciprocal Style: The coach defines the tasks, but teaching is done through a triad: the player who is active, a partner who gives feedback, and the coach who gives advice to both.
- Self-Check Style: The player rates his or her own performance (e.g., keeping records in a weight-lifting program).
- Inclusion Style: The coach arranges the exercise in such a way that players can choose their own level of difficulty. For example, in a shooting exercise, the player can decide whether to shoot a ball that is stationary, rolling, or bouncing.
- Guided Discovery Style: While there is still one correct way to succeed, the coach does not tell the players what it is. Instead, the coach poses questions to the players and allows them to "discover" the correct solution.
- Convergent Discovery Style: Similar to the Guided Discovery Style except that the players must come up with the questions as well as the answers. They decide the procedure for discovery.
- Divergent Production Style: The coach provides a question and the players determine how they will find the correct solution and what

the correct solution will be. The coach gives the players feedback on the quality of their solutions.

- Learner Designed Style: Similar to Divergent Production Style except that the players decide their own feedback. If they are satisfied with their solutions, that is enough.
- Learner Initiated Style: Similar to Learner Designed Style except that now the players also form their own questions.
- Self-Learning Style: Players are learning totally on their own. The coach is a bystander.

In the first five styles, the teacher/coach organizes the exercises and defines the goals. The players find solutions which the coach has prescribed to them. Most coaches fall most of the time into the dominant style.

In the next two styles, the coach poses a problem (e.g., a 2 v 1 attacking situation) and leads the players through exercises so that they find ways to solve the problem themselves. There is still one correct answer that the coach decides.

In the last four styles, the students/players find their own solutions to problems posed by the coach. The coaches give the players opportunities for both discovery and creativity. These styles can be difficult to use as the players can spend time doing things wrong and players must be self-disciplined and self-motivated. The learning that occurs in these last four systems is powerful since the players can feel a sense of satisfaction and ownership in having found solutions by themselves. For example, the Self-Learning Style is the equivalent of street soccer. The players determine everything: how they will play (the rules), how they will define success (the questions), and how they will succeed (the correct answers).

Each of these styles has positives and negatives. Important in all of them is how and when the coach gives feedback to the players. The coach can give the players feedback on their performance or only on their analysis of their own and their teammates' performance.

When a coach prepares training, he will use a certain teaching style, either intentionally or unintentionally. In order to maximize the benefit from it, he should think about the style he is using in advance. By thinking about the training style, the role of the coach and players in the training session, and by evaluating the session afterwards, the coach can not only be prepared but also improve his own work.

Different players will learn best in different ways. Different coaches will teach best in different ways. Different topics can be better taught in different ways. Coaches should be willing to experiment to find the exercises and methods that work best for their players.

Co Adriaanse, the former head of youth development at Ajax, added a personal view: "I always want to be able to do new things. This is essential for a Director of Youth Development at a club like Ajax. If the time comes when I realize that my function has become reduced to monitoring and maintenance, I will leave."[5] His sentiment is an important one for all clubs and coaches. The game evolves, and people who work in it must stay up-to-date.

Bearing in mind some important issues in coaching, let us review how the coaches work in the clubs that I visited. The numbers of coaches and other technical staff are in Chapter 2. In this chapter, the focus is on what the coaches do at training.

Coaching at FC Barcelona

Barcelona Technical Director Llorenc Serra Ferrer's style of managing his coaches is very organic. All of the youth teams have two coaches so that with goalkeeping coaches, the club employs 23 youth coaches, of whom six are full-time. While there are in-service sessions from time to time, Mr. Serra Ferrer works with his coaches on an open basis, getting involved at no set intervals. He also seems to know all of the players and stopped to give several of them advice during the week I observed. As a former professional team coach with Real Mallorca and Real Betis, he certainly has the experience to back up his words. As mentioned in Chapter 2, he also maintains a video and book resource center at the club so that the coaches can continue to learn and improve their coaching.

The coaches are required to have the National License of the Spanish Soccer Federation in order to coach at the club. From their education and experience, the coaches must handle the players' development not only from a technical standpoint, but also their tactical, physical, and psychological development. The coaches in Barcelona's "Football School" were not required to have any license qualification; they are young men starting their involvement with coaching.

As detailed in Chapter 4, training was well-planned. During my visit, the atmosphere at training was professional and intense. There was virtually no joking or laughing. The players concentrated fully throughout their training sessions. The coaches' and players' relations seemed to be very formal. The coaches became animated and loud at times, but they were never overly harsh toward the players. Perhaps their behavior reflected the national culture. While the environment within the club is as intense as one could expect, the matches the teams play are rarely competitive.

The players took a disciplined approach throughout the matches, even the team that I saw win 16-0. The Barça coaches, as a group, showed their commitment to their players through their passion. They seemed to have passed on to their players their intensity. The younger players seemed tense, perhaps as a result of their coaches' passion. There was no smiling or joking during training. Since the focus was there even in lopsided games it was not the match environment that was forcing the players to play well, but rather the environment created within the club.

From my observations of training, it seemed that the coaches wanted the players to "run the system" as much as to think (collectively) for themselves about how to solve situations in a match. The training corresponded to the dominant teaching style. Pattern play was the most popular form of training. The pattern play was a combination of technical work and learning the system. There were some training games with restrictions (e.g. each player allowed a maximum of two touches). All of the activities were clearly delineated by the coach and every player was expected to meet the standard he set. There was no room for the players to discover their own solutions to problems, let alone pose their own problems. Even in the scrimmages, the players had assigned positions which replicated their roles in a match. Especially since they were to "run the system" (see Chapter 4), the players could not create their own situations.

Most of the hands-on coaching, or teaching, that I saw was "coaching in the game." In other words, the coach would comment on what was transpiring: praising or criticizing what players had done. Between the coaching in the game and the dominant style of the coaches, there was only one way to play at Barcelona. While one can see the coaches devotion to one teaching method as limiting, there is power in being certain that all of the coaches, players, and teams are on the same page. Barcelona had the best record of developing their own players of all the clubs that I visited. The players they have developed are also top-class players by anyone's definition. Barça's success certainly shows the power of a consistent message from the coaches.

SUMMARY OF COACHING AT FC BARCELONA

- Barcelona's coaches ran the gamut of ages. The minimum requirement for them to coach at Barça was the RFEF National Coach's License. It was clear the coaches had a high degree of expertise in soccer.
- While coaching experience varied, Barça's coaches were all experienced as professional players also.

- The club maintains a video and book library for coaches. The technical director stays up-to-date on trends in soccer training and passes along information to the coaches.
- The Barcelona system is geared toward letting the training activities be the primary teacher. For example, when the players undertook some pattern play, the pattern "taught" the players a certain tactical idea.
- While the coaches displayed a lot of commitment and passion, it seemed to make the players tense. There appeared to be little enjoyment during training.

Coaching at Newcastle United FC

According to the English FA's Academy regulations, Staff (with required credential) must include: a full-time Academy Director (FA Academy Director License), a full-time Assistant Academy Director for ages under 9 to under 16 (FA Advanced Youth Coaching License or UEFA A Coaching License), a full-time Assistant Academy Director for ages under-17 to under-21 (FA Advanced Youth Coaching License or UEFA A Coaching License), a full-time physiotherapist for ages under 17 to under 21, a physiotherapist for ages under 9 to under 16 who is present whenever they are playing, a full-time Education and Welfare Advisor, an on-call doctor, a specialist goalkeeping coach (full- or part-time), and a sufficient number of coaches (all holding at least the UEFA B Coaching License) so that there is one coach for every ten players at every coaching session.

As outlined in Chapter 4, the Newcastle Academy's technical staff includes three full-time administrators who also coach, 20 part-time coaches including specialists in goalkeeping and conditioning, a scouting director, and two full-time physiotherapists. Some of the coaches at Newcastle United are still working toward the UEFA B Coaching License as the FA is allowing a grace period for this requirement since the Academy scheme is in its infancy. Most of the coaches already possess a higher license and have experience playing professional soccer.

The FA requires the club to hold two in-service workshops for the coaches each year and the FA itself also conducts two. The club's workshops tend to be specifically on technical football training, while the FA's are on various topics such as conditioning, psychological training, and other topics related to training.

In my opinion, one of the best attributes of the Newcastle Academy was the atmosphere at training. The players and coaches were able to laugh together. There also seemed to be a clear understanding of when it was not the time to joke and it was time to be serious. Also, despite the sometimes light-hearted atmosphere and talking to their coaches on a first-name basis, the players clearly maintained respect for their coaches at all times. The coaches were also willing to "put the boot in" when they felt it necessary. Perhaps as part of the frequent banter, the players did use profanity freely during training. I was impressed by how the players and coaches were able to balance joking with seriousness so that the atmosphere at training was lively and enjoyed by all. From this atmosphere, the players were able to see that their coaches cared about them having fun, but also learning the game and doing their best.

The atmosphere among the coaches is collegial. They work together informally, discussing soccer, training, and the development of individual players. The age of the coaches covered a wide range. The collegial atmosphere allowed the more veteran coaches to share their wisdom with newer coaches. Constant cooperation and communication is a necessity at the older levels as the players are frequently moving around among the teams. Mr. Irvine and his assistants meet every Monday to review the matches from the weekend and any other issues that have arisen. There is little other formal collaboration or evaluation. Coaches are not evaluated in any special way although they are observed regularly by the director and his assistants. The observations are more to stay in touch with the coaches and players, as well as to offer suggestions, than to evaluate the coaches. Mr. Irvine feels that the coaches must feel the freedom to coach as they see best without worrying about someone critiquing their every move.

While it is difficult to assess the commitment of the coaches during a one-week visit, the coaches that I observed were certainly enthusiastic during training. The players had a lot of responsibility at Newcastle, a measure of their coaches' faith in them. The players took care of their own warm-up and cool-down as well as their various jobs after training such as cleaning shoes and locker rooms.

Mr. Irvine has worked with several professional team coaches who have world-wide reputations. He reported that many of them spend training time keeping players fit, technically sharp with drill work, and playing under match conditions. These coaches feel that they should not have to work with the players on tactical preparation other than telling them verbally what the plan is. In these coaches' view, the players are professionals for whom they have paid a lot of money and if they cannot do the right things on the field, they will buy other players to replace them. Mr. Irvine and the other coaches in the Youth Academy at Newcastle feel this view is wrong. All players must have some training games at practice with conditions that will force them to see certain situations and make certain decisions so that they will be prepared to make them correctly in matches. From my observations of training at Newcastle, the coaches follow Mr. Irvine's philosophy. Drills are not enough and there must be some element of decision-making in training or else the players will not be ready to make the right decisions in a match.

There was a good mix of technical exercises, game exercises, and training games in the training activities. In the critical time between the technical exercises and the scrimmage at the end of training, the coaches used a variety of coaching activities and also actively taught their players. There was freeze-play coaching. The coaches would stop play to show players certain situations. There was a lot less of the "coaching in the game" commentary that occurred at other clubs. The players were allowed to play the game on their own. During some of the matches, the wind was so strong that the players would not have been able to hear the coaches if they had been yelling instructions to them.

The coaches at Newcastle used a variety of teaching styles. They not only addressed the group, but also took players aside to talk individually. The dominant and practice coaching styles were prevalent. Players were often praised for good decisions. A good decision was not necessarily the *only* correct one. The players were able to find their own solutions in scrimmages. Therefore, one could also say that the coaches were using the guided or convergent discovery styles. Newcastle had an excellent combination of different activities, different teaching styles, and enthusiastic coaches.

SUMMARY OF COACHING AT NEWCASTLE UNITED

- Newcastle's coaches are very knowledgeable. While not all of the coaches have the required license yet, many already have higher than required licenses.
- The coaches at Newcastle are highly experienced, both as coaches and players. Many were professional players.
- In addition to four formal in-service sessions each year, the coaches at Newcastle are students of the game. They talk to one another constantly about the game and about coaching it.
- As a group, Newcastle's coaches were probably the best teachers that I observed. They used a variety of activities and teaching styles. They also evaluated training sessions and matches afterward so that they could analyze their work and the work of their players.

• Through their enthusiasm, the coaches at Newcastle displayed their commitment to their players.

Conclusion

From my visits to the clubs (and talking with the coaches there), coaching courses I have attended, my own work as a teacher and coach, and a review of literature on coaching, successful youth coaches have five main traits:

1. *Knowledge*: of the game, of the developmental issues of youngsters, and of one's own individual players.
2. *Experience*: both as a player and a coach.
3. *A desire to keep learning*: about soccer and about coaching. As the game evolves, there is always more to learn.
4. *Ability to teach*: to pass along information to their players by various methods (individual players require different modes: demo, talk, key phrases, etc. Good teaching includes the ability to be flexible: taking into account the needs of the team and the individual players.
5. *Commitment to the players*: makes some of the criteria above work. Children work best with adults when they know that the adults care for them. Youth players can tell if a coach likes and respects them. If the coach and players have a good relationship, the players want to learn, and the coach is able to teach and to motivate. Being organized and enthusiastic are two ways to show commitment. After that it is more difficult to rate commitment because it comes down to relationships with the team and individual players.

KNOWLEDGE OF THE GAME

As their coaches have grown up in cultures where soccer was important and they have high standards for their coaches' credentials, the clubs that I visited have coaches with a lot of knowledge of the game. These coaches also know their players well. They see each other from four to seven times per week during the ten months of the season. The coaches also have access to support staff such as physiotherapists, coordination/conditioning trainers, psychologists, and nutritionists who can fill in gaps in their expertise.

EXPERIENCE

The experience of the coaches in the European clubs' youth programs is massive. Just by living their whole lives in a soccer culture, the coaches have lived with the game. The ages of some of the coaches indicated that they had been coaching for a long time. Also, a number of the clubs had former professional players, often from their own club, coaching their youth teams. Still, some of the clubs worry about the experience of their coaches because it is difficult to retain coaches when the work is part-time and the pay will not support a coach by itself.

CONTINUING EDUCATION

Continuing education among the coaches in European clubs was a mixed bag. For example, some clubs (e.g., Newcastle) had required in-service training every year. Barcelona maintained a video and book resource center for its coaches. Other clubs relied on the coaches working together and living in a soccer environment to keep their ideas fresh and up-to-date. As research in the game and training in it moves quickly, it is important for coaches to stay abreast of developments. Planning for continuing education, rather than leaving it to chance, is a good idea.

ABILITY TO TEACH

My observations of the coaches as teachers left me with some questions on two levels. First, drillwork and scrimmaging dominated training sessions that I observed. Second, "coaching in the game" seemed to be the most common form of teaching. While these are valid activities, there is more, much more, that a coach can do to help his players to learn. To my surprise, there was very little use of videotape, of either matches or training, as a teaching tool. To be fair, many of the training facilities predate the emergence of video technology so that filming from a useful angle would be difficult.

Ability to teach is critical for a coach. It is also important to note that a coach can help every player improve every aspect of his game. Awareness is a difficult skill to train. Yet, from testing done by scientists, it appears that players can improve their awareness. "Perceptual and decision-making skills can be developed through appropriate practice and instruction. Soccer specific measures of 'game intelligence' may prove useful as part of a holistic, multidisciplinary approach to talent identification."[6] As awareness is a characteristic for which the clubs look in a player, this finding is important. It is also an indication that players can improve everything about their games if their coaches will teach them.

Munich 1860 had a unique idea for working with players who might have gaps in their abilities. One of the physiotherapists at 1860 also had a coaching license and worked as the "individual trainer." During the week, he would take aside one or two boys at a time to work with them on specific technical issues. He worked with players who had been identified by their coaches as needing remedial work in a certain skill area. The director's requirement was that the individual trainer work with boys who were not in the School Pilot Project but were among the top players in the 1860 program. He feels that the players in the Project are receiving enough "extra" technical work. He also wants to focus the club's efforts on developing its best prospects. 1860 was the only club I visited that had an "individual" trainer. Similar to schools with "special needs" teachers or "learning specialists," 1860 has hit on a very educationally sound idea to help their players.

COMMITMENT TO THE PLAYERS

With only one week to observe each club, it was difficult to measure the coaches' commitment to their players. From what I did observe, enthusiasm certainly was not lacking. Even in the most casual atmospheres, the coach had the respect of his players.

It is also possible for a coach to be too committed to his players, to view a team as if he owns it. Coaches at European clubs did not move with their teams all the way through the youth program. At Newcastle, a certain coach stayed with a certain age group. At Glasgow Celtic, the coaches work with teams in two-year cycles. After working with a team for one season, a coach will move on with the team to the next age group. After the second year, they rotate back to where they started. For example, a coach might take the Under 12 team, move with them to Under 13, and then the following year, return to the Under 12 team and start the process again. At Bayern Munich, the coaches of the lower age categories (Under 12 to Under 8) work as assistants to the coaches of the older categories. This system removes the possibility of excessive zeal on the part of trainer to obtain success for "his team."[7] Keeping coaches with a team for only one or two years is yet another way in which the clubs try to help everyone involved keep perspective on working with their players so they develop, not so that they win.

The best coaching that I observed was at Newcastle United, followed by Glasgow Celtic. The coaching was the best because the coaches met the five criteria above and there was variety in the training, both in content and coaching style. The fact that the coaching in the two clubs I visited where the coaching was in English does make me worry that I rate them higher because I understood more. Still, I think I know enough Spanish, German, and Czech that I could get a sense for what the coaches were saying. There are also cultural issues. British culture is closer to American culture than Spanish, German, or Czech. Also, it was not so much what coaches said as how and when they said it. Most coaches did nothing more than organize training and comment on what occurred, telling players when they had done the wrong thing or they had not seen something. At Newcastle and at Celtic, in addition to being knowledgeable, experienced, and committed, the coaches were enthusiastic and positive. The latter two traits showed their commitment to their players. The coaches at these two clubs also engaged in the widest variety of types of training and teaching.

This is not to say that the coaching at the other clubs was bad, just not as good. For example, Mr. Prochazka at Slavia Prague was one of the best coaches I observed anywhere in Europe. From watching his teams play, it was clear they were trying to do the things he told me that he wanted them to do. He and his players seemed to enjoy training while he taught them the skills and ideas that were his objective. His training had a clear and positive effect on the way his team played.

Before I visited the clubs in Europe, I expected to find brilliant coaches everywhere. I was surprised to find that while they were knowledgeable, experienced, and organized, they were not necessarily great teachers. With the time and money (for things like coordination training or enticing top players) that European clubs throw at their youth programs, they are able to turn out players. It shows that all coaches can learn from coaching and educational research.

Notes

1. Kormelink and Seeverens, p. 72.
2. Cook, pp. 12–25.
3. Kormelink and Seeverens, p. 71.
4. Williams, Alty, and Lees. "Effects of Practice and Knowledge of Performance on Skill Acquisition," reported in Andy Grant's "World-wide Review of Science and Football Research: The Fourth World Congress in Science and Football, Sydney," in *Insight*. Issue 1, Volume 3, Autumn 1999. Published by The Football Association, Potters Bar, Hertfordshire, England, p. 19.
5. Kormelink and Seeverens, p. 75.
6. Williams et al., p. 25.
7. Buzek, Mario, and Rudolf Psotta. "Youth Training Abroad," in *Fotbal a Trénink* March, 1997. Noesis, Usti nad Labem, Czech Republic, pp. 5.

Chapter 6

Philosophy of Youth Soccer in Europe

Of course there is space for the exceptional. But you have to see it first. That's one thing. So you have to see it, and then you have to give it room to develop. And then let a player develop so that he discovers himself. Because people ... have to develop through shame and getting things wrong. We used to have those boys play two teams higher than their age level and we put them ahead of other players on purpose. At the higher level, they got kicked so hard that they really understood. I believe in a very hard school. Then you get to the next stage: turning playing football into the mentality of winning. Then you see that a lot of players fall by the wayside. Why? Because few people have taught them how they could bring higher returns on their qualities. Quality football is one thing, but how do you get the maximum return on that quality? Because that's what it's all about in soccer.

— Johan Cruyff [1]

Changes in society have forced European clubs to place more emphasis on their youth development programs. In many parts of the world, street soccer is almost extinct, like many other street, playground and sandlot activities. With a lot of cars in the streets, it is not safe to play in them. Many parents, fearing for their children's safety from criminals, are reluctant to let them just go out and play. In many areas of the United States, people build housing developments without sidewalks. They assume people will drive anywhere they go. It means people who live in this type of housing expect to go to an activity, not just go out and play. With sedentary options such as television and computers, it is tempting for children not to go outside at all. Organized youth soccer then takes on two roles: developing soccer players (who might not play at all unless they are in an organized program) and helping children be physically active and learn more about themselves and how to relate to others. The most important role of youth soccer, and of youth sports in general, is to provide an opportunity for young people to grow.

Of the clubs that I studied, Bayern Munich, Glasgow Celtic, Newcastle United, and Munich 1860 have put increased emphasis on their youth programs in the last five years. It signals recognition on the part of the clubs that they must do a lot of work to develop players that they might not have had to do in the past.

If the clubs are going to work seriously with children, they must answer for themselves a number of questions. What are their underlying philosophies and goals? Are their activities and the atmosphere in harmony with their stated goals? How do they address some of the sticky issues around youth player development? Are they as hard-nosed in their approach as Johan Cruyff?

These questions are critical. The clubs must perform a balancing act between development of the youngsters as players and as people. While a lot of training can help in both areas, there are also conflicts. Time is one example. If the players are at the club all afternoon everyday, they have little time to do their schoolwork. It remains a paradox of youth development that on the one hand the atmosphere must be intense and competitive so that the players will have to work hard and learn, and, on the other hand, there must be an outlet for the players to have fun and to grow as people.

All of the clubs that I visited had clear conceptions of what they were trying to do. They had a philosophy of youth training. Some spend time thinking about their philosophy. Others created a philosophy based on the training they wanted to conduct.

Having looked at the nuts and bolts of the youth development programs in a number of European clubs, it is now possible to see how they rate as places for children to develop as players and people. One might suggest that European clubs' philosophies should be the first topic of this book, not the last. After all, the clubs have certain goals in mind when they start their youth programs and a certain philosophy that dictates how they run the programs. I have put philosophy at the end of the book so that we can compare what the clubs do with what they say they are trying to do. We can see how their activities and atmosphere match up with their stated goals.

Similar to previous chapters, I have highlighted two clubs as case studies: Glasgow Celtic and Munich 1860. For each club's youth program, I will look at the philosophy and goals, the level of harmony between the stated philosophy and the activities and atmosphere that I observed, and how they tackle the difficult issues in youth development. After the case studies, there are brief descriptions of unique aspects of the philosophies of the other clubs that I studied. There are then three sections that evaluate European clubs' philosophies in general: the stated philosophies and goals of youth programs, observations on whether their activities and atmosphere match with their stated philosophy, and how they tackle the difficult issues in youth development. The chapter concludes with a summary of the important ideas in the philosophy of youth development in European soccer clubs.

Glasgow Celtic: A Family Atmosphere

PHILOSOPHY AND GOALS

Like most clubs, Celtic wants to develop as many players as it can for its first team. As reported in Chapter 4, they also want to do more for their youth players than teach them to play soccer.

When I asked Celtic's Head Youth Coach, Willie McStay, about the family atmosphere at the club, he agreed it did exist. As reported in Chapter 4, it is definitely a family affair for him, as he, his brother, his father, and his son are all part of the club. There were other indications of the family atmosphere. The players and parents from the teams eat meals together on Monday nights after the boys have coordination training. The coaches were all enthusiastic and friendly with their players. At the same time, the coaches did lay down the law when they felt it necessary. There was a noticeable bond between the coaches and their players.

OBSERVATIONS OF ACTIVITIES AND ATMOSPHERE

Given the atmosphere, it seems Celtic's activities and their stated goals are in accord. They are developing players for their first team and they are maintaining a good balance between professional development and personal growth.

The youth training program at Celtic is comprehensive and modern. In addition to its soccer coaches, the club has physiotherapists, a sports psychologist, a sports physiologist, a strength and conditioning coach, and a nutritionist. All of these people help ensure that Celtic leaves no stone unturned in their effort to train professional soccer players. The Celtic coaches work within the club and in Scottish soccer as a whole to help discern the future of youth training in the club and in the country.

The club takes responsibility for their players' development as players and people. There are numerous examples of the club's concern for their players. They provide the full-time youth players with vocational training. They provide all of their players with nutritious meals. They give the players tasks, such as cleaning the locker rooms, so they can learn about responsibility. They pay a boy's school fees for one year after he leaves the club. All of these examples indicate that Celtic goes above and beyond requirements of a soccer club to provide an experience for their players that will help them grow as people and become professional soccer players.

DIFFICULT ISSUES

As with any competitive youth program, there are some difficult issues. The club brings in 16-year-olds as full-time players. It is a very young age to commit to a profession, especially a risky one like soccer. The club has young boys almost literally lined up to join it so that staying in the club is very competitive. The club must temper the individual competition with building team work and self-confidence so that players are not "looking over their shoulders" all the time. The players must learn to become "winners" (especially against arch-rival Glasgow Rangers). It becomes difficult to maintain the balance between winning and having fun. Celtic must strive to maintain balance in its work with its youth players.

Celtic balances intense and comprehensive training with other aspects of its youth program that helps the youngsters develop as people, as well as players. As mentioned above, the club has activities such as schooling, homework support, meals, and meetings with a club psychologist to ensure that the players have a well-rounded experience. Also, the atmosphere in the club is such that the players are having fun while they are working hard at the game.

Craig Brown, Scotland's national team coach and technical director, told me he was not satisfied with the work the clubs in his country did to develop players. For example, he pointed out, they play too many games. It is easy to write his comments off as typical federation versus club complaining. After all, Celtic and all Scottish clubs are involved in working with their federation to talk about the future of youth training in Scotland. However, Mr. Brown's comment does point out that perspective is important in one's evaluation of youth development. Celtic's priority is to develop players for their own senior team so that it will win games. Mr. Brown's priority is to develop players for the whole of Scotland so that his national team will win games. While someone from the federation might have a larger view in mind, their goals seem similar in the end to those of the club. If an articulate spokesman for proper youth development, like Craig Brown, has reservations about a youth program, it shows that one must constantly monitor youth programs to make sure they are being true to their philosophy.

Summary of Philosophy of Youth Training at Glasgow Celtic

- Celtic is trying to develop as many players as it can for its first team. The club staff members acknowledge that they must do more than simply train soccer players. They have boys in their care and they must help them to become young men.
- One would have to say that the clubs' training activities are in accord with their philosophy. The training is intense and modern in the interest of developing players. At the same time, the mood at training is open to having fun. The players and coaches are enthusiastic. As in any family, there are times when an authority figure must put his foot down. The atmosphere was conducive to development as a player and a person.
- Celtic does a fine job tackling the difficult issues in youth development. Their program goes well beyond what is required. While they do expect boys to be full-time players after they turn 16, they provide them with some education, meals, and even housing if necessary.

Munich 1860: German Engineering

Philosophy and Goals

1860's youth sector exists to develop players for their first team. At this time, the club has no set target for the number of players that it wants to produce annually. They do expect to produce more and more players in the coming years as their recently energized youth program (with the School Pilot Project outlined in Chapter 2) matures and brings its full effect to bear on the players' development.

1860's approach to youth development is thoughtful and comprehensive. The youth director, Ernst Tanner, stays up-to-date on developments in the game and in coaching. For example, the players undergo very modern fitness training and testing (see Chapter 4). The club also recognizes that it is dealing with children, not miniature adults. There is an emphasis on making training fun. Mr. Tanner has turned down players who wanted to come to the club because they would have had to travel too far every day to attend training. He will only allow strong prospects to stay in the club's boarding house. If he does not believe strongly in a player, he does not want to uproot him from his home life. The club does not want to interfere in a boy's education. They want to keep a balance between soccer training and personal development.

OBSERVATIONS OF ACTIVITIES AND ATMOSPHERE

Perhaps the most impressive part of 1860's youth set up was that they have clearly put their philosophy into action. For example, they know that they must keep the game fun to keep their players interested and enthusiastic. Therefore, the School Pilot Project contains a small-sided games component so the players can simply enjoy playing. The club is also the only one I visited in which the players are encouraged, and even taken by their own coaches, to play other sports. The Under 16 coach, Ernst Thaler, told me how he takes his team regularly for in-line hockey, basketball, and other sports so that they can regenerate after a match, enjoy some time together as a team, and just have fun. As Mr. Tanner summarized, the club likes to use other sports for variety, enjoyment, and also to help boys improve their over-all coordination.

In training, there were exercises which had a serious point, and were fun for the players. For example, one team played keep-away with an American football. Another team played a game in which every player had to link arms with a team-mate. There were a number of spectacular spills and bizarre goals. Fun was definitely designed into a lot of the activities of the youth teams.

The training in 1860's youth sector was, of course, clearly designed to help players become professionals. From watching 1860's youth training, one could not expect to find more comprehensive and intensive youth training.

DIFFICULT ISSUES

1860 tries hard to address some of the difficult issues in running a youth program. 1860's training schedule takes into account the school schedules of the players. They all complete secondary school. As explained in Chapter 2, 1860 and some other clubs have taken on the task of working with schools to provide extra training for their young players in their School Pilot Project. In these ways, 1860 avoids the difficult task of asking their players to leave school before they have graduated.

1860 displayed sensitivity to the need of young children to have fun with the game. While training accomplishes all of the goals that its role demands, the club also tries to make sure that the players have fun while they are doing it. It did surprise me therefore to see two different teams in which there was one coach on each sideline during matches. Being under the coaches' commands during a match surely takes away from the enjoyment for the players.

The club also helps players it is releasing to find new clubs so they can keep alive their dreams of playing professional soccer. With teams for players as young as seven years old, helping to find a new club may not be enough. Such a young player is sure to be dazed by being told he is no longer welcome. 1860 and Barcelona were the only clubs with players so young. At Barcelona, the players are signing up for a one-year program, Barça's intramural football school, without any real promise of being in the club after that. At 1860, the youngest players are already in an elite team and can see that many players do continue to play in the club as they rise through the ranks. Releasing players is never easy, but 1860 has a very difficult situation.

Interestingly, in a discussion with Bavarian regional coach, Reinhard Klante, he said that the clubs in his area *were* primarily interested in winning youth matches and not in player development. He mentioned one German club (not 1860) which discouraged its players from playing for the Bavarian regional selections because it was beneath their dignity. Mr. Klante coaches the regional select team so that he too has a team that he wants to see be successful. However, the regional select team is strictly for viewing top players so that his motive of player development seems pure. If someone like him had criticisms of top-flight youth programs like 1860, it is worth listening. Similar to the comments of Craig Brown above, Mr. Klante's comments show again that perspective is important.

SUMMARY OF PHILOSOPHY OF YOUTH TRAINING AT MUNICH 1860

- 1860 has put a lot of thought into how they will achieve their goal of preparing their youth players to play in their first team. They want to keep the boys' enthusiasm high while training them intensively and not interfering with their schooling.

- 1860's training activities and atmosphere are true to their goals. The training is comprehensive. At the same time, the players are enjoying themselves and receiving their educations through the end of secondary school.
- By arranging their youth program so that boys can finish school, 1860 avoids one sticky issue. While the players are business-like on the field, the club organizes activities so that the players can also enjoy their training and other activities.

Ideas from Other Clubs

FC BARCELONA

The atmosphere of the youth training at Barça was professional. The technical director wore a suit and had a big office with a secretary. The standard of formality he set carried down to the youth teams. Even amongst the youngest teams, there was little or no joking during training. The coaches were passionate. The matches of even the youngest teams at Barça had several hundred spectators. There were as many as a thousand people watching the Under 18 team's league matches. These spectators followed the action closely, referring to players by name. Their intensity seemed to carry over to the players. The atmosphere was more intense than at other clubs. The atmosphere at the club really brought home the paradox of youth development: it must be competitive so that the youngsters will develop as players but still take into account their having fun and developing as people. Watching grown men with no affiliation to the players barking at 12-year-olds, I wondered if perhaps the atmosphere for the youth players at the club was too intense.

BAYERN MUNICH

Werner Kern, administrator of Bayern's youth program, says, "We can't promise their parents that one day they'll play professionally for FC Bayern, but we can promise that they won't neglect their studies." Adds youth director Bjorn Anderson, "Players are bound by one simple rule: If a player falls behind in his studies, he doesn't play. A player who can't keep up in school or on the job can't be expected to give a hundred percent on the field either. It's up to us to teach our players discipline, good conduct, and ambition. Strength of character is the best thing we can give them."[2] By tying a player's academic performance to his training, the club is trying to bring together the goals of youth training: personal growth and playing growth are important at the same time. In this case, the scales are even tipped toward personal growth since the player cannot play without keeping his schoolwork in order.

NEWCASTLE UNITED

As at other clubs, the goal of the Newcastle United Youth Academy is to develop as many players for the first team as possible. This goal means training them not only to play soccer well but also to handle big events and to develop the self-discipline required of a professional player. All aspects of the activities in the Youth Academy were geared toward preparing the players to be professionals. Indeed, Mr. Irvine's personal goal is to see all of the players who come under his charge become professionals, if not at Newcastle, then elsewhere. The Newcastle coaches were the most clear, of all the ones with whom I spoke, about the need to train their players as *professionals*, not just excellent soccer players.

The atmosphere at training was terrific. The players and coaches were enthusiastic. As at Celtic, there was a lively banter amongst the players and coaches. The light-hearted atmosphere seemed to occur naturally from the players' and coaches' senses of humor.

Newcastle also stood in contrast to some other English Youth Academies that had bought players from around the globe. One club reportedly had spent £5 million ($8 million) on players for its Under 18 team. That club seemed more interested, therefore, in buying players than in developing players. At Newcastle United, without saying it in words, the coaches' attitudes made it clear that they took seriously their charge to develop players not only for Newcastle, but also for England generally.

SLAVIA PRAGUE

The youth sector at Slavia receives very little guidance from the club's hierarchy. Mr. Prochazka, the youth chief, said he would like the club's general manager to give him a goal for the number of players that he expects the youth sector to produce. He wants the club to put more emphasis on its own youth players rather than first looking outside the club for new players for their first team. He felt that if club officials gave the youth sector a target, they would consider Slavia youth players for the first team before looking outside, rather than afterward. In other words, Mr. Prochazka would like there to be more pressure on his youth department to develop players. Of course, such additional pressure would eventually trickle down to the youth players. Increasing the pressure, and therefore intensity, for youth players is not inherently a bad thing, but it must be handled carefully. Too much pressure is not good for youngsters' development as players or people.

Evaluation of European Clubs' Philosophies

Philosophy of youth development is a matter of setting priorities. These priorities are apparent in several ways: stated philosophy and goals of the club's youth department, observations of the activities and atmosphere of the club and its teams, and the ways that the club handles difficult issues in youth development.

PHILOSOPHY AND GOALS

The first questions regarding the issue of training young soccer players are: "Why do European clubs have youth programs? What are their goals?" The very structure of the European clubs is the basis for their philosophy. They all want to develop players for their first teams. The youth teams are supposed to be a feeder system into the professional team. There are side benefits such as good publicity. Now more than ever before, the clubs need to train players if they are going to have high caliber players. Even if they do not end up developing their own players, they are adding to an environment that will hopefully produce players. Some clubs have specific goals for their youth program. For example, Bayern Munich's goal is to provide seven or eight players for their first team at any given time. At Ajax Amsterdam, the goal of the youth development staff is to produce three new players for the first team every two seasons.[3] A club can also have specific training goals. A club might want to develop players who are good dribblers. I have addressed specific training goals in Chapter 4.

While their record of developing professionals is very good, the European clubs' record for developing players for their own teams is mixed (see Chapter 3). European clubs' mixed record of developing their own players does raise the question of why have a youth program at all? Perhaps their money would be better spent by donating it to the youth departments of smaller clubs and obtaining rights to the players that the smaller clubs produce. The conventional wisdom is that clubs are saving money on transfer fees by developing their own players, that they are developing players who understand the club's philosophy, and that they are developing players who care more about the club and therefore winning at the club. There is some evidence that clubs are not saving money. In the book *Winners & Losers: The Business Strategy of Football*, the authors (Szymanski and Kuypers) cite their statistical study in which there is no correlation between having "home grown" players and winning, once one allows for wages.[4] They also point out that youth policies are "expensive and speculative." They cite several reasons for this belief. Investing in training and human resource management are expensive in any industry. Youth programs are speculative in that players may fail to develop, or they may develop and go to another club.[5] Manchester United has dominated English soccer in the 1990s with a team that is loaded with players who came through the club's youth system. Even in this case, the authors are not convinced. "The case of Manchester United is not convincing for two reasons. First, most big clubs develop a high share of their own players. Second, when Manchester United began their dominance in the early 1990s, their team was almost entirely made up of players they acquired through transfers."[6] If the authors' analysis is correct, one must ask what the point of having a youth program is for a professional club.

I believe there are several reasons why the clubs might still feel the usefulness of having a youth sector. First, players must develop somewhere. Professional clubs have the resources to put into youth development. If they are not developing players for their own team, they are developing professional players and creating an environment in which they can challenge players and produce top-class ones. The coaches at Newcastle United were very clear that they saw part of their charge to develop English players as a whole. Second, Alan Irvine, the Newcastle Academy director, said he thought Alex Ferguson, the Manchester United coach, would dispute the findings of Szymanski and Kuypers. He would probably argue that having a lot of players from the Manchester United youth program has meant more success for his team. Mr. Irvine added that those running a youth program are content to turn out solid professionals with the hope of unearthing a real gem for the club from time to time. If a club spends $1 million annually on its youth program, as Newcastle does, it will take the club several years to spend as much money as it might on buying a top-class player.

Finally, while few clubs' youth directors stated it explicitly, perhaps there is value for the boys in the program just by being part of it. Given the low rate at which they do produce their own players, the clubs must be satisfied with providing a growth experience and helping turn boys into young men. I certainly hope this is the case, since ultimately the kind of people developed in these programs is more important than the kind of soccer players. As highlighted in Chapter 4, most clubs do a good job considering a player's personal development in addition to his technical development.

OBSERVATIONS OF YOUTH SECTOR'S ACTIVITIES AND ATMOSPHERE

One can also tell a lot from the types of training the clubs undertake and the atmosphere at the club. If the medium is the message, then the players are learning as much, if not more, from their environment than they are from the stated philosophy of the club. The people in the club must ensure that the activities and atmosphere in the youth sector are in accord with their stated goals.

Inevitably, activities are somewhat influenced by the amount of money available. Because the clubs that I visited were large and relatively wealthy, they were able to spend a lot of money to ensure that their soccer training was first class. They were able to stay up to date on trends in the game with specialists such as conditioning coaches. They were able to buy any necessary equipment and have access to whatever facilities they wanted to use.

Some clubs stated that personal growth was also one of their goals and others did not. Regardless, in most of the clubs that I visited, the clubs were after well-rounded professional players. Because of this philosophy, the clubs did take into account the players' personal development. Most clubs undertook activities to ensure that there was fun in the game and that the players were able to maintain their studies.

Clubs undertake many activities to help their players grow as people. For example, they provide homework support for their players. At Ajax Amsterdam, the club has 14 tutors and the players stay at the club after training to complete their homework. Barcelona has a tutor in its dorm. Celtic provides homework assistance one night each week. The clubs also want the players to learn about responsibility. At many of the clubs, the players have certain jobs assigned to them: cleaning, caring for equipment, and polishing soccer shoes. A job system can become abusive, but at the clubs where I saw it in action, the coaches handled it with sensitivity so that the players were learning about responsibility without feeling tortured. Glasgow Celtic sent their older players to meet with a sports psychologist each week. The clubs all said it was important to have well-rounded individuals on their teams. While the level of follow-through on this sentiment varied, all of the clubs did something to help their players grow as people, as well as players.

Atmosphere is more difficult to evaluate than activities because it involves a lot of personal feelings. It is difficult to be precise about atmosphere. One can draw conclusions from training and matches. Are they highly structured or mellow? Do the parents and other spectators rant and rave? Do the coaches and clubs emphasize good sportsmanship? There is also a lot to be learned from observing the behavior of the coaches. For example, how do they interact with the players and referees?

The general mood during training ranged from very formal at Barcelona to very informal at Slavia Prague. All of the clubs had atmospheres that were defensible both as proper environments for youngsters and as reflections of their philosophy. When they were watching training, parents were largely silent while the players and coaches worked. At games, the parents did not mix with the players during the matches, although they would cheer for them. Other than the occasional complaint, I did not see any red or yellow cards for coaches or players for arguing with the referee.

During training at the different clubs, the best coaches modulated the atmosphere from light-hearted to very serious based on where the team was in preparations for its next game. Only at Barcelona was the training highly intense in every moment. During games, the intensity was higher. My view was that the coaches considered the games like teachers giving a test. The emphasis was on playing well, not on winning. The maddest at his team that I saw a coach was after his team had won, but not played as well as he thought they could have.

Generally speaking, the activities and atmospheres of the clubs were in line with their philosophies. Particularly the atmospheres at the clubs were different. Just as different people prefer different educational styles or types of schools, they can also prefer different atmospheres in a club. One critical component in creating the atmosphere is how the club handled the difficult issues in youth soccer.

The Difficult Issues in Youth Soccer and Player Development

Whether they realize it or not, the European clubs that I visited have tackled the difficult issues of youth player development to greater or lesser degrees. Some of the difficult issues are explained below. For example, at what age must a player commit to playing soccer full time and leaving school? How does a club balance fun and personal growth with the highly competitive environment that youth development requires? The answers to these difficult questions are what determines whether a club is a proper environment in which a youngster should spend his important developmental years.

Balance is a difficult issue for clubs to consider in their youth development programs. For example, clubs must balance the soccer specific training of a player with aiding the player's personal growth. With the monetary stakes in success so high in professional soccer, how do clubs reconcile the corporate investment side of their youth programs with the care and development of young boys? How do the clubs keep the fun in playing for the kids when they need to develop competitors and winners? Can clubs re-create the spontaneity and joy of "street soccer" in an organized "work" environment? In the end the key questions are, what is the purpose of the youth program? What are its goals?

A related question is when do youth players have to give up both school and soccer? In some countries (e.g., Scotland), players must decide when they are 16. In others, players finish secondary school (Spain, Germany) and must decide at age 18. In the United States, college is the preparatory league for many sports, so players can decide at age 22, possibly holding a college degree when they do. When is a young man old enough to make this difficult decision?

Another difficult issue is the releasing of players. Before I visited the clubs in Europe, I was worried that they would chew up and spit out their "raw materials," or youth players, if they felt they were finished with the players. While they certainly do drop players, my experience was that they did not chew them up or spit them out. All players in the programs received benefits from playing in it. When a player was released, one of the coaches met with him and his parents to explain why it was happening. Then the club helped him find a new place to play. Methods of releasing players are one of the difficult issues in youth soccer and youth sports in general, but the clubs that I visited were as compassionate as they could be. Tolerating compromises and the balancing act that clubs must do is necessary if clubs are going to create an atmosphere in which top players will be produced.

In writing this book, I have taken for granted that developing the best soccer players we can is a valuable goal. It is a big assumption. In Europe, soccer holds a cultural position such that there is no question that youth development is important for professional and national teams. In the United States, this position is not as clearly cut. Major League Soccer is not guaranteed to be around forever. Even the U.S. national team has a difficult time attracting crowds, and often a majority of spectators will root against them at home matches. The United States is in the difficult position of having to attract people to the sport as well as manage the sport.

The issues outlined above are important ones. There are certainly many other important philosophical, or difficult, issues for people involved in youth soccer to consider. Nothing is more important for the future of the world than how it develops its young people. Of course soccer is a small component in the overall development of the world's youth. For kids who play, soccer can be a terrific environment for learning about themselves, for learning how to work with others, for being physically fit, and best of all for having fun. Because these issues are so important, they certainly merit more than a few paragraphs. I have included them here so that all people involved in youth soccer, coaches, administrators, referees, and even players, will keep them in mind and try to keep perspective on what we are doing. Whether one keeps them in mind or not, one takes a stand on them by the way he runs his team, club, league, camp, or other program. In my opinion it is better to think about them. It is better to be proactive and plan your program so that you can be sure it sends the messages to the players that you want them to receive. Ultimately, the lessons a player learns about himself and the way he develops his character are the most important issues in youth soccer or almost any youth activity.

Conclusion

From each club's philosophy and priorities, it is clear that their priority is to develop professional soccer players. Each club has a tone, either by design or by happenstance, which they believe is conducive to creating a professional player. They take, for the most part, a holistic approach to developing their players and they take the time to be thorough. While the European clubs are not without some problems (e.g., selection and cutting of 7–10 year olds at some clubs, coaching from both sides of the field at a game), by and large, they are doing the right things for their players. That is, they have highly trained coaches, who work with their players in all areas of their development, and have enough time to make a difference. The question I started to ask myself was: would I want *my* son in this program? In almost every case, the answer was yes.

It is important to note that European youth coaches have an advantage over American youth coaches in seeing an incentive to develop players, rather than win. Because the professional teams in Europe are part of clubs, with the youth training departments, they can dictate that the priority is to develop players. In the United States, MLS entrants are teams, not clubs. They have no youth training departments. It means that the millions of youth teams in the United States are left to their own devices to follow their own priorities.

Philosophy, or perhaps we should call it perspective, was the biggest difference I saw between youth soccer in Europe and the United States. The clubs in Europe have clear goals in mind. As explained in previous chapters, the clubs also have a clear vision of how they go about achieving those goals. Few clubs or teams in the United States have a stated philosophy, but perhaps they can learn from the European clubs. In the next chapter, I will make suggestions, based on my experiences in Europe, for youth soccer coaches in the United States.

Notes

1. Barend and Van Dorp, pp. 223–24.
2. *FC Bayern Munich Junior Team.* On Compact Disc.
3. Kormelink and Seeverens, p. 60.
4. Szymanski, Stefan, and Tim Kuypers. *Winners & Losers: The Business Strategy of Football.* Viking, London. 1999. p. 180.
5. Szymanski and Kuypers, pp. 286–87.
6. *Ibid.*

Chapter 7

Recommendations for the United States from European Clubs

It's a game of ideas.
— Graham Ramsey, Coaching Director,
Maryland State Youth Soccer Association

The United States is not the Czech Republic, Germany, Spain, or England. We cannot say, "We'll do it just like _____." (Fill in the blank with your favorite soccer-playing country.) We can learn from all of the countries mentioned above, and many more, but we have to pick and choose from their youth soccer programs what will work in the United States. From the information in previous chapters, coaches, administrators, and parents can look critically at what European clubs do and try ideas from them to improve the training of young soccer players in the United States.

There are millions of ideas in soccer. What is important is to consider ideas—about training, about coaching, about every aspect of the game—and to try the ones that appeal to see if they improve the players and improve the game. Below, I have outlined the ideas that I think would help us in the United States.

The structure of this chapter parallels the structure of the book. The sections include: organization, facilities, and equipment; player evaluation; training timetable and components; coaches; and philosophy. At the end of the chapter are concluding remarks.

Organization, Facilities, and Equipment

ORGANIZATION

The structure of European clubs has many advantages. Because the youth teams feed into one another and eventually to a professional team, it is possible for the club to maintain a single, coordinated philosophy of soccer education through the club. The training can follow a curriculum through a season and over the several years a player might be in a club. Because all of the teams fall under the club's operation, the club can pool resources for equipment, facilities, coaches, and other staff (e.g., physiotherapists). Coaches are in an environment where they work closely with other coaches and they can watch each other work. The club's administration can control the quality of the coaches. The club can also move players to older age groups if their development calls for it. The organization of European clubs is helpful to their mission.

While an American "club" might have a similar number of teams to the clubs in Europe, very few have the same overriding structure. Players are not really part of the club, but rather members of individual teams. American clubs rarely dictate how the training of various teams is structured. American clubs are unlikely to change their structure to match that of European clubs. We can, however, try to use some of their organizational ideas. For example, American clubs can appoint (and some already have) coaching directors. While these people might not enjoy the authority over the club's coaches that they might in a European club, they can hold seminars from time to time to make sure that certain ideas are floating around in the heads of the club's coaches. Even though American youth soccer clubs are not like European ones, we can still learn from them on a multitude of topics.

There are a number of possibilities for improving American youth soccer's requirements for organizing a club and affiliating professional teams with youth teams in a more European-style club. Currently, youth soccer teams must be part of a club that is affiliated with USYSA through their state youth soccer association. The only requirement for the club is that it do some paperwork. USYSA could demand that clubs have certain people or programs. For example, it could insist on a coaching director responsible for providing a certain number of coaching seminars to the club's coaches each year. The English FA has clear guidelines for professional clubs that want to have youth programs. USYSA can also make guidelines for youth clubs to ensure the quality of their programs.

Some lower division American professional teams have affiliations with local youth clubs. These are arrangements to sell tickets for the professional team's games to the youth players and their families. In return, the professional teams often hold clinics for the youth players. The clinics could be expanded into regular coaching. Eventually, these relationships could approach the organization of a European soccer club. It is my opinion that this will work better with lower division, such as the United Soccer League's A-League or D3 Pro League, clubs since they are often community-based.

The work of the Munich clubs in forming partnerships with local public schools is also an excellent idea. Local soccer clubs enter into arrangements with public schools in their areas. Such partnerships would be new to the United States and would face many hurdles. For example, coaches working in the schools would have to have some kind of educational certification. The benefits to the youngsters would be great. Such partnerships are worth pursuing.

FACILITIES

Facilities in the United States are not better or worse, but only different from those of professional clubs in Europe. For example, locker rooms with showers are standard in Europe, both at clubs and at public parks in Europe. The professional clubs in Europe do spend a lot of money to maintain their fields and a lot of them use artificial turf extensively. Many clubs in Europe also have fitness centers with a gymnasium and weight equipment. Americans have access to all of the same amenities although they are organized differently. For example, school teams usually have all of the facilities of a soccer club. We also have parks with soccer fields and health clubs with weight equipment. As I have mentioned previously, many of the best players in the history of the sport played in diabolical conditions until after they became professionals. While facilities are not the most important issue, there are three ideas we can take from Europe that might help our players.

The first facility idea is regarding field maintenance. The clubs took good care of their grass fields. They rotated the use of them so that no field was overused. They also spent the money on proper care: watering, seeding, rolling, etc. Consistency of field surfaces, whether artificial or real grass, was important. It was important for the development of the players, so they could control the ball properly. As more and more soccer parks are built in the U.S., we should consider surfaces for them that we know we will be able to maintain. While coaches will always look for the best facilities they can provide for their players, excellent facilities alone will not create top-class players.

The second facility idea involves the use of artificial turf. While the ultimate cost savings of using artificial turf are not clear, there did seem to be some advantages to training on it. The quality of the surface is reliable. A coach does not have to worry about if the field will be bumpy. A couple of the clubs had artificial turf fields that had the "shaggy grass" that played very much like real grass. The long blades held up the ball like real grass and the surface was softer than traditional astroturf. People at the clubs with artificial turf also said that the technology is moving rapidly and they expect to see the surface continue to improve. In areas of the United States where the climate makes it difficult to maintain a nice grass field, this type of field would make a lot of sense. I would certainly like to see natural grass remain the field of choice. However, if it is too difficult to maintain a proper grass field, artificial turf is better for teaching the game than a "grass" field strewn with bumps, holes, or clumps of grass.

The third idea is regarding locker rooms. The changing rooms with showers that are prevalent in Europe are a good idea for two reasons. First, young players should practice and learn about proper hygiene. If we want to develop well-rounded people, they should learn about taking proper care of their bodies, including keeping them clean. Second, time spent together, playing or not, is at a premium for a team. If players have more time together, they have more time to build team spirit. As people in the U.S. build soccer facilities, they should include changing facilities. Of course, there are more important things, like coaching education, on which to spend money, but if we are building new soccer facilities, we should build them right.

EQUIPMENT

Like facilities, equipment is not a critical component of player development, but also like facilities, the right equipment can help. Americans have access to all of the same equipment as the teams in Europe. Of course, the European clubs are able to save money by buying equipment for several teams to share. Also, because European clubs often have training centers, the equipment is stored near the training area. In the U.S., the coach or a parent brings the equipment to training, and there is a limit to how much a car will hold. Few American clubs buy equipment for their teams to share or have their own training facility.

Coaches should ensure that they have a way to do coordination and conditioning training with their players. One need not buy all the fancy athletic equipment. Like Slavia Prague, one can make one's own athletic equipment. Filling tires or bottles with sand is a way to make "weights" or "medicine balls." Corner flags can be used as poles for agility work. The important thing is not to buy the equipment, but to find a way to do the coordination training. It was an important element of the overall training at every club that I visited.

In most clubs that I visited, coaches pumped up the soccer balls to absolute rock hardness for training. Players would not use them unless they were totally full. Barcelona was the only place where they were not pumped totally full with air. It has an effect on what the players can do with the ball. A rock-hard ball is more difficult to control and kick, so must improve players' skills. Equipment is an easy target for player development, especially as so many other American sports are so equipment-laden (e.g., American football, ice hockey, baseball). Because equipment can be bought, it is easier to focus on than something more difficult to achieve, like improving skill. It is important to remember that as long as one has some kind of ball, everything is possible in player development.

Player Evaluation

Given their experience and rate of identifying players, European youth clubs provide some examples for those running youth teams in the United States. There are five key lessons for Americans from the European clubs. They are about tryout system, recruiting radius, player characteristics, methods of evaluation and retaining players, and releasing players.

TRYOUT SYSTEM

Most of the clubs that I visited observed players several times with their own teams, then bring them in for a trial period of a few weeks. Watching players on their teams, rather than in the artificial environment of a mass tryout gives them a fairer chance and gives the scout a more realistic picture of the player. The trial period also lets the team's coach see how a player fits, or doesn't fit, into the team. By using such a system in the United States, we can be more sure than we currently are that players are receiving a fair and thorough evaluation.

RECRUITING RADIUS

In England, clubs cannot take players younger than 16 years of age who live too far from their training ground. In this way, they can ensure that players are not spending so long in a car that they are neglecting their schoolwork. By enforcing a similar rule in the United States, we can also ensure that players don't neglect their schoolwork and that they are at training as often as they should be.

PLAYER CHARACTERISTICS

The coaches and scouts at big European clubs like the ones that I visited have a lot of experience evaluating players. While the traits they look for in a youth player do not provide certainty that a player will make it to be a professional, their experience suggests that they are experts in evaluating young talent.

In general, they look for the following characteristics (in no particular order):

- Athleticism: Speed especially is an important athletic skill for which scouts look.
- Awareness: Scouts look for players who can see and react to the game around them. It does not mean they are necessarily looking for players with a lot of tactical understanding, only players who can see the game.
- Attitude: Every coach wants hard workers. Aggression and courage are also characteristics for which scouts looked.
- Technical Ability: While coaches can do more work to improve a player's skill level, a good starting point always helps. Players who can make the ball do what they want always catch the eye.

While these characteristics are not really anything new, European coaches' interest in them does reinforce their importance.

EVALUATING/RETAINING PLAYERS

European clubs believe on-going evaluation is important, just like in school. The coaches at the clubs I visited sat down with their players two or three times each year to review the performances. For younger players, up to 15 years old, the parents were also present for the evaluations, which included a written report. American coaches should have formal and regular evaluation sessions with their players. "Report cards" are a great source of information and motivation. American coaches also need to motivate players to remain interested in the game. European coaches saw maintaining players' interest as important, and they are not faced with as many competing sports as American coaches are. We do have small financial incentives such as scholarships or paying for a player's equipment. Offering these types of external motivation is not as powerful as nurturing a player's internal desire to play well.

Releasing Players

When a player was released at the clubs I visited, the coach met with the player face-to-face and explained why the player was being released and what he needed to do to improve. European clubs also helped a released player find a new team if he was interested in one. American youth players deserve the same consideration. Handling the release of players with sensitivity can help the player see that the game still has value for him, even if he is going to a new team. If the release of players is not handled well, it can be a turn-off for new players who might be interested in a certain team or club. Whether we are picking (and releasing) the right players or not, we must ensure that we treat the players we have with respect and give them the best training that we can.

Training Timetable and Components

Training Timetable

Time is a big issue in youth soccer. When "street soccer" was prevalent, time and the game were the main teachers. Whether one likes it or not, planned training sessions and coaches are now part of the development equation. The season in Europe lasts approximately 40 weeks. Weekly training ranges from two or three sessions for the youngest players up to six for the oldest, Under 18, players. European youths play a lot more in a learning environment than their American counterparts.

Weekly Training

The training week is structured carefully in European clubs. We would do well in the United States to emulate their weekly training cycle. In a typical week, the schedule works backwards from the game on the weekend. Training is modulated through the week so that the players can recover from the previous match with light work early in the week; they do their heavier work during the middle of the week, and then taper off their work late in the week in preparation for the coming match. There are always one or two days off during a week, usually the day after a game and in the middle of the week. For older teams, there are one or two days each week with two training sessions. The weekly training timetable of Barcelona in Chapter 4 is representative of the amount of training in a European club. It is important to train, to play in a learning environment, but it is even more important that the time be spent on the right things.

LENGTH OF SEASON

American youth teams can do pretty well in terms of the length of their season, but the older teams do not train as much each week as their European counterparts. If a youth team does not play all winter or all summer, cutting their season to 20-25 weeks, they are not playing enough. Our players must play more soccer if they are going to develop at the same rate as European youth players. A coach must also remember, though, to seek the balance between playing enough to become a top-class player and not neglecting school work or other activities needed for youngsters to become well-rounded people.

The length of the playing season raises the difficult issue of when to specialize in one sport, since playing 35-40 weeks per year means little time for active involvement in other sports. In America, we have long praised the "three-sport athlete," and some European clubs acknowledge that it is better for their players to be involved in more than one sport. While a longer playing season would undoubtedly mean better soccer players, there are costs involved. The length of a player's season is also affected by school sports.

The school soccer teams in Europe are recreational, not developmental. Given the resources and enthusiasm surrounding high school and college athletics, we must be sure we use school teams to our advantage in the development of players in the United States. School sports have been instrumental in the development of other American sports. We must find their proper role in the development of soccer players. High school and college soccer kept the game alive for many years in the United States. The status of the game has changed now. Club soccer has become the main development ground for American youngsters. Those kids playing high school soccer and club soccer at the same time are ultimately begging for trouble in terms of physical and psychological burnout. Just like elite high school basketball players play on outside teams, soccer players must also play on club teams in order to play enough to develop to their potential.

A three-month per year season in any sport is not enough to develop an elite player. Just as basketball players play their club ball in the spring and summer, soccer must find a way to mesh the schedules of high schools and clubs. Otherwise, high school soccer will be a hindrance to developing players. High school soccer teams must also limit their schedules to one or two games per week. Many high school players are caught in a trap where they are constantly playing games and being asked to perform. During a high school season, many players are competing constantly and they need more developmental training time. While many American players need to play more soccer to develop at the same rate as their European counterparts, it needs to be in a learning environment, not just a competitive one.

College soccer faces a real dilemma. There are many outstanding college coaches who are knowledgeable about soccer and committed to seeing their players develop as players and people. However, the college season is just too short for players to have enough time to develop to their full potential as players. The current NCAA rule is for a total of 21 weeks of soccer per year. Because other college sports, primarily American football and basketball, are the primary developmental track for those sports, college athletic administrators assume that it is so in every sport, so they limit out-of-season play. Even if the college players play for ten weeks in a league during the summer, they are still playing less than their European counterparts. Players of similar age at clubs in Europe are playing for ten months or more per year. College football and basketball work well as the minor leagues because they have longer seasons than soccer. Colleges, through their organizing body, the NCAA, want their basketball and football teams to be the developing ground for future professionals because of the money they earn from them. Of course, college should provide the balance between professional development and personal growth for athletes as it does for engineers, economists, and other professionals. To put the American system in a European context, colleges can be thought of as a division 2. Players are free to leave if they are wanted by division 1 (the professional teams). Of course, in the U.S., they are drafted instead of bought, but the secondary league principle is the same. Students with other areas of interest are also free to leave the university before they earn a degree to pursue their professional careers. The problem for college soccer is that the season is not long enough for the players to develop as well as they might.

Unless college soccer can bring in the massive revenue that college basketball and football do, the season is not going to get longer. There is also the question of whether colleges should be the developing grounds of future professional athletes. That model has certainly led to a lot of problems in college football and basketball in terms of players not working toward degrees and receiving illegal payments. To their credit, MLS and USSF are working together to bring young players into the Project-40 program so the players can train with MLS teams to develop as players without going to college. The Project-40 program sets aside money for the players to go to college after their careers are over. Other than college money being put aside for retirement, Project-40 has no formal program for mentoring young men as they try to become professionals. Young players also take a bigger risk than their European counterparts when they join Project-40. They receive lower pay and they also have to hope that MLS stays in business. I believe we need to do a better job of preparing our players through age 18, and we need to do a better job of working with them as they make the transition, in every way, from youth players to professional players.

Training Components

The one word which sums up the training of the professional clubs in Europe is "holistic." The coaches consider every part of the player's development: psychological, physical, technical, and tactical. The clubs also take care of the whole person, helping their academics, as well as their soccer. A number of the clubs stated outright that they wanted to develop well-rounded professional players, not just very good players.

Even if we do not develop European style clubs in the United States, coaches can carry out well-rounded training. We can pay more attention to the physical and psychological/social elements in training. More training time would help, but it is possible to make the training that currently exists more efficient. For example, a coach can make coordination activities part of the warm-up. There are examples of coordination training in Appendix D.

We could also use a more thoughtful approach to the training emphases at different ages. American clubs rarely have a technical director who can dictate guidelines for training to the coaches. Just as schools plan curriculum through many years so that it follows a sequence, American soccer clubs can do the same. Individual coaches can use activities and introduce ideas that are age-appropriate and follow a preplanned order. Players then receive a comprehensive and systematic education in the game.

SYSTEMS OF PLAY

I encountered three schools of thought on systems of play for youth teams. Some clubs did not give it a lot of thought so that individual team coaches were able to pick their own formation. The youth directors in these clubs were of the opinion that players need to learn the game and not to play in a certain system. At some of these clubs, a team might switch formation from game to game. The second method was to have all of the youth teams play in the same system. In the case of Barcelona, the teams played in one of two similar systems. The thinking here is that the system encouraged certain activities (e.g., 1 v 1 attacking or zonal defending) that the club wanted to emphasize. It also made it easy for players to understand their roles in the team. The final school of thought was a mixture of the first two. 1860 Munich had different predetermined systems of play for each age group. Their youth director was of the opinion that players do need to play the game, not a special system, and that therefore he wanted them to be comfortable with different systems. At the same time, he recognized that different systems provided different emphases and that it was useful to play different ways at different ages so that the different systems would emphasize certain age-appropriate activities for the players.

I believe 1860's philosophy was the best. Systems of play are important in that they provide a forum for learning the game. One system is not inherently better than the others. Different formations and the different positional requirements can emphasize certain parts of the game. Therefore, it makes sense to use different systems so that players can emphasize certain characteristics. For example, if a team plays with wingers, those players will have a lot of opportunities to attack 1 against 1. If the team plays with zonal defending, the players gain experience with that aspect of play. Coaches must give thought to what their system of play is teaching their players, to ensure that it emphasizes the parts of the game they want it to emphasize. The system is a developmental tool.

COMPETITIONS

The competition in which players play is also a developmental tool. The competition must have characteristics that help players learn. For example, in Europe the emphasis is on league play, not tournaments. Developmentally, it is a better approach. There is a premium on consistency. It is also okay to experiment since one game is rarely going to make or break a season.

The competitions are also an extension of training. Winning is only important in that it gives some indication as to the team's and the players' progress relative to their peers. The games are primarily learning experiences. Coaches analyze their players' work on a "test" and see what they need to improve.

Coaches

From my observations, coaching is an area in which the Europeans are not too far ahead of the United States. The main reason is that many of the coaches I saw in Europe were organizers only, and not teachers. The big difference between American coaches and the European coaches I observed is that we do not have as many knowledgeable coaches in the United States. From observing coaches in the United States and Europe, there are also some gaps in the education of American coaches, which I will highlight below. There are five key traits of an excellent coach: knowledge of the game and of coaching, experience in the game as a player and coach, desire to continue learning about the game, ability to teach, and commitment to his players. Below are suggestions for helping American coaches in each area.

KNOWLEDGE OF SOCCER AND OF COACHING

Because soccer is a relatively new sport in the United States and does not dominate the sports scene the way it does in other countries, American coaches are rarely in a "soccer environment" their whole lives, as most Europeans are. As the game continues to grow in popularity in the U.S., lifelong learning through simple exposure to the game should improve. Even so, my impression is that we have coaches who know the tactics and techniques of the game, but have difficulty putting them across given the limited training time with which they work. My experience is that American coaches need to learn more about training players' physical abilities. American coaches are not necessarily doing the wrong drills. Of course, one can always learn new and better drills. However, we can do more with the drills we have in terms of the teaching a coach does during a drill. As stated above, if we have more time to train, we can add more training exercises, including proper physical work.

In order to ensure that coaches know the game and all of its components, coaches must be trained. The courses are in place in the United States, but they are not comprehensive enough. If we are going to require coaches to seek certification, we must be sure that the certification means something. Of all the countries I visited, the courses in the United States are the shortest and have the least-qualified instructors. Because the American courses are relatively short, there are fewer topics, and the ones that are in the course are not taught in as much depth. When I told the youth director of one of the European clubs that I visited that there was little or nothing in U.S. courses about exercise physiology or fitness training, he started laughing and said that it was such a basic topic, he did not understand how a top-level course could not include it. A good first step would be for those in charge of coaching education in the United States to visit the courses in other countries and compare their top courses with the ones in the United States. In the United States, we must be open to ideas about the game from places that have more experience and more success in the game than we do. American coaches must also be sure they understand the influences of the many ethnic groups, particularly Hispanics, on soccer in the United States. All of the coaches I met in Europe were eager to share ideas with others. We should take advantage of their willingness to share ideas about the game and about coaching education.

In American society, coaches are the ones with primary responsibility to develop better players and to keep a balance in developing them as players and people. Especially if youth coaches are going to earn large sums of money, they should be held to a high standard of professionalism: expertise, behavior, and results in terms of player improvement, not wins. Youth players have passes which help to ensure they are the right age and that they only play on one team. The USYSA could use passes for coaches to ensure that they cannot coach more than two youth teams at the same time. Surely any more than two would mean the coach would miss games or practices regularly. USYSA should also establish minimum criteria for coaches' education. Every club in every country I visited had high requirements for the education of the coaches of even their youngest players. Our players deserve as much.

EXPERIENCE AS A PLAYER AND COACH

Very few American coaches have experience in professional soccer, as players or coaches. Of course, it is not their fault, since there have been few opportunities for Americans to play professional soccer until recent years. For example, we have had national team coaches whose first experience with professional soccer was coaching the national team in the World Cup. Perhaps this lack of experienced coaches is the reason that MLS teams frequently hire coaches fired by other teams rather than look for new coaches. Hopefully, MLS and the U.S. players abroad will be able to contribute to U.S. coaching in the future. It takes time for experience to come. With so many Americans gaining professional experience, the U.S. is on the right track toward gaining coaches who have a lot of experience.

DESIRE TO CONTINUE TO LEARN

USSF has tried to tackle this problem with its Continuing Education Unit program. NSCAA has its annual convention and other activities. Even if these activities had little to offer in and of themselves, their usefulness in bringing coaches together to talk about the game is important.

As with the coaching courses, we must ensure that these programs and other continuing education activities are of high quality. It means we must look at ideas about the game from all sources. For example, a track and field coach would have useful information for soccer coaches. An educator with information on teaching styles would have useful information for soccer coaches. Coaches from different backgrounds and different countries can also help with new perspectives on the game.

The Maryland State Youth Soccer Association (MSYSA) has started a helpful program for coaches' continuing education. Each summer, MSYSA holds a number of "International Weeks." For these weeks they bring in coaches from around the world (e.g. Holland, Brazil, Ireland, Czech Republic). The weeks are for players and coaches. By bringing in these coaches, they are exposing the coaches and players in attendance to new ideas about the game. Coaches are free to accept or reject the new ideas as they please. The important thing is that the new ideas will stimulate their thinking about the game. The program in Maryland is an excellent model for continuing education in coaching. Hopefully, more programs like Maryland's will enable coaches to continue to learn more about the game.

The library of videos, books, and magazines that the technical director of Barcelona maintains is an excellent idea. Some clubs and state youth associations have similar arrangements. Every club should make these resources available for their coaches. If the club does not have a suitable facility, local libraries will often take donations of such items. The library will then take charge of storage, maintenance, and circulation.

ABILITY TO TEACH

The overall coaching in Europe, while it was good, did not differ as much as I expected from coaching in the United States. It was in the area of actively teaching the game that European coaches were not particularly impressive. Even in the Czech coaching course, while there were classes on teaching methods, there were no practice-teaching or sample training sessions as part of the exam. A lot of the coaching in Europe was primarily organization. Teaching is an area in which American coaches can catch and even overtake the Europeans.

Coaches must use different methods to actively teach the game to their players. Imagine an English teacher who simply gave the students an assignment each class and then watched them do it, perhaps critiquing their work from across the room if the student made a mistake. The students might figure out eventually how to write well, but it would take a long time. Picture a swimming instructor who tells the nonswimmers what to do, sends them into the pool, and then yells advice and encouragement while they founder. If one is coaching experienced swimmers, it might work, but with new swimmers, a new approach might be required. As outlined in Chapter 5, there are many ways for a coach to reach his players. Coaches do need to create a training environment in which the players will learn from the game. Coaches also need to ensure that players have feedback on their play and to *show* players how to perform skills and make decisions. If coaches are actively teaching, their players will learn more about the game. At the same time, coaches can be too active and not allow their players to have fun, to explore the game on their own, and to express their creativity. Teaching requires a fine balance between allowing players the freedom to explore and providing the structure within which they can learn. If a coach can find this balance, it is one way to show players his commitment to helping them improve.

COMMITMENT TO THE PLAYERS

If players are going to have a positive experience in youth soccer, they must know that someone values their participation. Even if a player is marginal, he can find value in playing from the cameraderie of the team, the physical exercise, the fun, or other aspects of playing. For a player to realize a feeling of value in playing, he must feel valued by his coach.

There are a lot of ways a coach can show the team his commitment to it. First and foremost is to attend all of the games and training sessions. Bayern Munich was the only club I studied where the coaches trained more than one team. The coaches of the younger teams at Bayern worked as assistant coaches for the older teams. At every other club, coaching more than one team was simply not an option. A coach cannot be spread so thin that he regularly misses team activities. The Bayern example suggests that a coach can handle two teams at once. Surely training any more than two would mean that the coach cannot show the commitment to his players that they deserve.

A coach's behavior when he is with his players also indicates interest in them. In Europe and the United States, I have observed coaches talking with players, sharing a laugh, and many other things to show that they care. Helping youngsters to feel valued in any activity is important. It is worthwhile for all coaches to keep this idea in mind.

Philosophy

PHILOSOPHY AND GOALS

From my observations of top-level youth programs in Europe, it is possible to strike a balance for youth players among having fun, developing as a player, personal development, and learning to compete (trying to win). While the European clubs have their critics, their clearly stated goal is to develop professional players for their first teams. Of course, the teams try to win their games, but not at the expense of developing well-rounded professionals. In addition to becoming strong soccer players, the players must learn about the importance of responsibility and hard work. Even in an atmosphere as competitive as the youth departments of top European clubs, they were interested in more than developing someone who could only play soccer well. American youth teams would do well to consider their priorities and then plan their activities accordingly.

DOES STATED PHILOSOPHY MATCH ACTIVITIES AND ATMOSPHERE?

European clubs turn out more top players than American ones. The biggest difference in their training is that the time they spend playing is much more purposeful than the time the kids in the United States spend playing. We must make sure that our youth teams' activities match their stated goals. One way to ensure the priorities of our youth teams are correct is to make sure the coach is in charge. Every club that I visited had guidelines for the parents of their players: where they were and were not allowed to be and how much "encouragement" they could give the players during training and games. This approach implies that coaches will have the correct perspective. Perspective and balance in youth soccer should be a topic in coaching courses, and coaches should be held to high standards, not just of soccer knowledge but also as educators of children.

Another way to keep harmony between what we want to do and what happens is to monitor closely the forms of competition. For example, we could limit the number of matches a player is allowed each year to improve the ratio of training to matches.

If we are to develop better players in the United States, the most important change is to change the attitude of the adults who coach or manage youth teams. They must find ways to emphasize long-term goals like player development rather than short-term goals like winning a game or tournament.

TACKLING TRICKY ISSUES

Working with children is an awesome responsibility. Their whole lives are in front of them, and one wants to make sure they are able to achieve what they want with their lives. At the same time, the experience should have value even if it is in an area a child does not eventually pursue. In youth soccer, players should have a valuable experience, even if they are not going to turn into professionals.

To ensure that everyone has benefits from playing, we must ensure that there is balance in the objectives and activities of youth soccer teams. Learning to compete and developing as a player are important. As players improve their abilities and hone their competitive edge, they will want to win, as a sign that they have developed as they think they have. We must make sure that the desire to win does not interfere with other goals, like having fun and developing as a person.

The European clubs that I studied had clear stances on the difficult issues in youth soccer. A coach must think in advance where he stands on such issues as how competitive to make a team, whether he will allow absences for nonsoccer activities, and if he will demand that a player's school grades are acceptable. Reasonable people can disagree on how to tackle these and other tricky issues. What is important is that everyone understand beforehand what kind of program they are joining.

Coaches of elite youth teams are usually hired by the parents. Coaches must make their priorities clear to the parents. If the parents have one set of expectations and the coach a different set of goals, there will be discord that will ultimately hurt the children's experience. Coaches and parents must be teammates. By letting parents and players know what is expected of them and what the goals of the team are, parents and or players are free to choose other teams if their interests are not the same as those of the coach. While different solutions to difficult issues are possible, coaches should ensure that parents and players understand the program up front.

Regular meetings with the players and parents to reiterate the priorities of the team are a good idea. Communication is vital to a good youth soccer experience, for all parties involved.

Conclusion

Because soccer is a game of ideas, there are limitless possibilities for how to play and how to train. There are good ideas about soccer all over the world. If a coach wants to develop top class players, one must consider different ideas and decide what is best for him and for his players.

In the United States, we have many advantages, but also many challenges. No other country is as wealthy or has as diverse a population. Few other countries are physically as large, have such a range of climates, or as many popular sports that compete with soccer. Every coach must be true to himself and take into account his environment. Within that environment, he can choose ideas from other countries and adapt them to his own use.

My experience in Europe was that coaches there are always learning from those outside their own country, whether they realize it or not. Because players and coaches move so easily from one country to another in Europe and because of the internet and satellite television, coaches have exposure to many different approaches to the game. This book is meant to do the same thing: expose coaches in the United States to ideas about the game from around Europe.

I hope this book and the ideas in it will help everyone to improve the youth soccer experience of their players. Even if we do not develop better soccer players, we must work together to ensure that children in youth soccer have an experience that will help them grow as people.

Appendix A

Questionnaire About Youth Soccer Development Programs

Philosophy

1. Why do you have a youth program?
2. What are the goals of your youth program?

History

1. How long has your club/federation run special programs (teams/clinics for players under the age of 18)?
2. How did the youth program begin (changes in society, recognized need, influence of coach, and/or competing with others)?

Overall Set-Up

1. How many teams do you have, at what ages?
2. How many players on each team and how many on the field?
3. What competitions (if any) do your teams enter?
4. How often do they play matches?
5. How often do they train (is there a regular weekly training schedule)?
6. How many coaches does each team have? How many youth coaches does the club employ? Full-time? Part-time?

7. What are the qualifications for the coaches?

8. How are the coaches allocated (for example, do the best coaches go with the youngest or oldest players or do coaches stay with one age group year after year)?

9. Does the club have other trainers (physiotherapists, fitness coaches, nutritionists, physiologists)?

10. What facilities do you have at your club (fields, gymnasium, fitness center, locker rooms, administrative offices, schools, etc.)? Are any of the youth teams training outside of the club's main training area?

11. What equipment do you provide players?

12. What is the total cost of running the youth program for one year?

Training Methods

1. Are special balls used for different ages?

2. How does the emphasis change over time for technique and tactics?

3. Do all of the teams play the same system?

4. Are there certain training exercises used?

5. When do specialized physical and mental training come into use?

6. How do youngsters learn to compete?

7. Are players engaged in other sports, or are other sports used as training tools in any way?

8. Do your youth players have duties or opportunities other than playing (ballboys at 1st team matches or boot polishing for example)?

9. To what extent does the club care about the youth players' schoolwork?

Player Discovery

1. What are you looking for in a youth player?

2. How do you identify players for your youth teams (try-outs, scouts)?

3. How is the player pool refreshed?

4. How and when are players weeded out?

5. How and when are new players brought onto an existing team?

6. How do you deal with recruiting players from other clubs? What are the incentives for the player? How are relations handled with the other club?

7. In a typical year, how many players from your oldest youth team do you sign to professional contracts in your club? How many typically sign with other professional clubs?

Federation/Club Collaboration

1. Are there requirements of the federation regarding the experience of youth players (U-21 spots on the first team roster, maximum number of games)?

2. Are there conflicts regarding the players' time (e.g., call-up to national teams)? How are they resolved?

Miscellaneous

1. Can you give a brief outline of the coaching license program in your country?

2. Is the first team manager involved with the youth players in any way?

Introduction to Training Exercises

The training exercises in the appendices represent samples of the development activities that I observed in Europe. There are examples of:

- Warm-up routines in Appendix C
- Physical Training in Appendix D
- Technical Training in Appendix E
- Tactical Training in Appendix F

It should not surprise you to learn that none of these exercises are earth-shaking. There is no "magic drill" that will automatically turn youth players into world-class stars. Player development is a long process.

There are numerous books full of training exercises and drills. The point of this book is not just what happens at training, but *why* it happens. The activities are here because they are interesting, they fill the needs of the clubs that use them, and they can be useful for coaches looking to expand their arsenal of exercises for their players. They also illustrate how the clubs that I visited try to develop their players according to their own philosophies. Perhaps one of them will help you put across a new idea to your players.

More important than the exercises is what happens in them: the effort and behavior of the players and coaches. A coach must use training exercises as a means to teach. An exercise can go a long way toward helping players, but the coach must maximize the learning in an activity by being involved.

The drills, as I have described them here, are not written in stone. In fact, I encourage all coaches to look at them and adjust them to your own players.

Efficient training is also important for a coach. Every exercise has a physical component that can help a player's physical qualities in addition to training some other part of his ability to play. For example, the pattern play in the exercises of FC Barcelona also provides numerous repetitions for technique development. Indeed, some exercises for training one realm could easily fit into another one also.

The descriptions of the drills include the following information (when applicable): playing area, number of players, organization, description, rules, scoring, type of exercise, variations, and coaching points.

A few other notes: The sizes of playing areas are given in meters. Meters are only slightly longer than yards and may be thought of as the same for the purpose of these exercises.

Rather than join the debate about whether "drill" or "training exercise" or "training environment" or some other term is right for the activities in soccer training sessions, I have used the terms interchangeably.

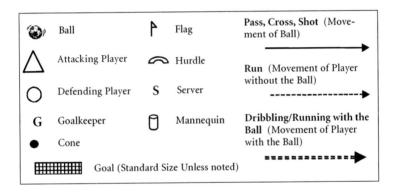

Figure B1. Key to symbols in diagrams

Warm-Up Routines

The following warm-up routines come from two sessions led by Mario Buzek, one the instructors of the UEFA "A" coach's license course in Prague. I have described them below in full. It is possible to take certain activities from them as part of another warm-up.

Full Body Warm-Up Routine

The warm-up routine is useful because it warms up the whole body, not just the legs. For all of the activities, players work with a partner and they have one soccer ball between them.

1st part: Moving across field and back, partners are five meters apart:

- Jog, toss ball back and forth
- Move sideways, toss ball back and forth
- Jog, bowl ball back and forth
- Jog, toss ball to partner, then overlap (run behind) him
- Move sideways, basketball bounce pass to partner

2nd part: Standing ten meters apart, throwing the ball:

- Throw-in with exaggerated back bend, backward and forward
- Underhand toss with two hands
- Overhand throw with one hand (baseball throw)
- Shot put
- Standing backwards, touch ball to ground, then throw over head with both hands
- Hard bounce pass so receiver must jump to catch

3rd part: Standing back to back:

- Twist trunk to alternating sides passing ball at waist level
- Twist trunk to alternating sides passing ball at ankle level
- Pass ball over head and between legs

4th part: Five meters apart:

- Sitting, toss to player's side for "dive"
- On knees, toss to player's side for "dive"

Warm-Up Routine for a Training Session with 1 v 1 Duels

Each player has a partner and the team is in a 20 meter × 20 meter grid. The players do not use a ball for this warm-up.

- Tag: the player who is not "it" can only shuffle his feet. The player who is "it" tags his partner by head-butting him in the chest.
- Tag: the player who is not it can only run backwards
- Partners jump together and bump chests
- Partners jump together and bump shoulders
- One partner follows the other around the grid, doing various exercises (e.g. touch the ground, jump, etc.)
- A central area is marked in the grid 5 m × 5 m. One partner tries to block the other's path into the central grid by moving his body into the other player's way (see Figure C1).

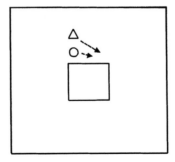

Figure C1. The defender tries to block the path of the attacker into the center zone.

Warm-Up for the Day Before a Game

Willie McStay, the Head Youth Coach at Glasgow Celtic, believes that for a warm-up there should be no soccer balls or else every player should have one. If there are just a few balls, the players tend to begin kicking them over long distances or shooting before they have warmed up properly. Mr. McStay led the warm-up below on the day before a game. Therefore, the point was not only to warm up for training but also to bring out the players' enthusiasm so that the team spirit would be good leading up to the match.

The warm-up began with the players doing five minutes' jogging back and forth across the field on their own or in small groups. By warming up gradually on their own, they can prepare their bodies and their minds for training. The second activity was individual ball-juggling for ten minutes.

The third warm-up activity took place in a 20 m × 20 m grid. It lasted five minutes. Each player had a ball and dribbled around the grid. At the coach's signal, the players would leave their ball and take possession of a new one. As the players looked for a new ball, the coach would kick one of the balls out of the grid. The player who ended up without a ball had to do a light penalty (e.g. five "jump-ups"). As the game progressed, players without balls stayed in the grid and continued to move. On the next signal, all the players looked for a new ball. The coach added the rule that anyone who stopped moving while the players without balls were doing their penalty had to sprint once around the grid. The idea was for the players to stay in constant motion.

The next activity also took place in the grid. The players juggled their soccer balls and, on command, left the ball to do certain exercises: skipping, jogging with high knees, alternating short and long strides while jogging, and other similar forms of running. After five minutes of this exercise, the players stretched for eight minutes.

The final activity of the warm-up was a series of relay races over a 20-meter course. The team was divided into four groups. There were five races:

1. Dribble out the 20 meters, then chip the ball back to his teammate. The teammate had to be able to catch the ball in his hands behind the starting line.

2. Juggle out, catch the ball in his hands and half-volley it back to his teammate.

3. Juggle all the way out and back.

4. Dribble out, flick it up to his head, juggle the ball three times with his head, and chip the ball back to his teammate.

5. Dribble out, pick up the ball and toss it high in the air, do a somersault, catch the ball again before it hit the ground, and half-volley it back to his teammate.

In each relay, the players had to complete them properly or start again. Due to the competitive nature of the activities, the players had a lot of fun. Even the penalties were given out and done with a sense of humor. At the conclusion of the relay races, the players' enthusiasm was high, both for the main part of training to follow and the game the next day.

Appendix D

Physical Training

Physical training was the area of biggest difference I saw between the youth programs of Europe and the United States, particularly coordination training. The physical training that the European clubs use comes from analysis of the game and the activities of a player during a game. From observation, video tape analysis, and heart rate monitors, the European coaches, with the help of sports physiologists, have analyzed in great detail the physical demands on a player during a game. Knowing the physical demands on a player, the coaches can design fitness tests to see how well their players' fitness levels compare with what is required in a game. From their analysis and the fitness testing, the European coaches have designed physical training programs for their players.

Age-appropriateness is particularly important in physical training. Training six-year-olds like adults may not help them learn to play soccer and could even be dangerous for them. If kids who have not developed strong bones are lifting weights, they can seriously injure themselves. Growing youngsters should not be lifting weights until they are at least 15. Physical training for the youngest players should be entirely coordination work: agility, balance, coordination, and flexibility. Finally, the first priority for training young players should be learning ball skills rather than physical training.

It is also important to recognize that players grow and develop at different rates. Vaclav Bunc, physiologist at the Charles University in Prague, believes that every team should have at least three groups for fitness work. By using different groups with different workouts, players have a physical training program which is more tailored to their individual needs.

Fitness Tests

I saw several different fitness tests. While they involve some medical or fitness expertise, they do make it clear that there are better ways than distance runs to test players' fitness levels. At Munich 1860, the players have aerobic fitness tests twice each year. The players run 1600 meters on a running track four times, at increasing speeds each time: 3, 3.5, 4, and 4.5 km/h. The players hear a series of beeps that keep them on pace. A nurse takes a small blood sample before the first run and after each run so that the blood can be tested for lactate concentration. In this way, 1860 can maintain an accurate record of their players' fitness levels.

At the Charles University in Prague, scientists do similar fitness testing, but in a laboratory using a treadmill or exercise bicycle. Players also wear heart rate monitors so the physiologists can have a complete picture about what is happening to a player's body as he undergoes physical activity. For example, the *aerobic* fitness test at Charles University is done on a treadmill. It is tilted 5 percent to simulate the wind resistance an athlete would feel running around a track. The warm-up phase is two "runs" of four minutes each. The first at 11 km/h and the second at 13 km/h. After brief rest, the player does a continuous run on the treadmill starting at 12 km/h. The speed of the treadmill is increased each minute. In addition to testing the blood and heart rate, they also test the players' breathing for oxygen use.

The researchers at Charles University also do an *anaerobic* fitness test to determine a player's ability to reproduce bursts of speed. After a warm-up, the player pedals for ten bouts lasting five seconds, with 30-second rest periods in between each bout. The different fitness tests show the need to think about how we test fitness in the United States.

Coordination Training

"Fast Footwork" Training

As detailed in Chapter 4, Monday night is Glasgow Celtic's physical training night. All of the youth teams up to Under 16 undertake physical training only. The Under 12 "Fast Footwork" session lasted 70 minutes. It was held on the rubberized track surface around the field in the main stadium of the club.

Warm-Up (15 minutes)
As it was a cool evening, and the team had played a match the day

before, the warm-up was lengthy. The benefit of being in the stadium was that the players were out of the wind and rain. The warm-up consisted of jogging and walking. While walking, the players did various arm rotation exercises. They also stopped periodically for stretching.

Main Part (45 minutes)

The main part of the session involved the players moving through a set course that was 40 meters long (see Figure D1). After five meters at a jogging pace, the players would make one movement through a ten-rung "agility ladder" followed by two meters of jogging. Their next movement was through seven "mini-hurdles" (approximately 15 cm tall), then two more meters of jogging, followed by another movement through the second speed ladder, two meters of jogging, and running the final ten meters at ½ speed (faster than jogging). They would then walk back to the start for their next movement. The players each made 41 movements through the course according to the sequence in Table D1. Throughout the time, the coach constantly reinforced running and or moving with proper technique: keeping the back straight and lifting the arms and knees. As the players had done these exercises before, their technique in doing them was very sharp. During the session, two trialists arrived and joined the group. Their participation made the regular players' excellent movement skills clear.

Figure D1. Under 12 coordination training course

	Table D1 Exercises Through the Coordination Training Course			
Movement Number	*Number of Repetitions*	*First Ladder*	*Mini-Hurdles*	*Second Ladder*
1	4	run forward	run forward	run forward
2	4 (2 on each side)	sideways along ladder, place both feet in each rung of ladder, one at a time	hopping forward with both legs	sideways, both feet in each rung of ladder, one at a time
3	1	hopping forward with both legs	slalom	hopping forward with both legs

Movement Number	Number of Repetitions	First Ladder	Mini-Hurdles	Second Ladder
4	2	hopping forward on one leg	hopping forward with both legs	hopping forward on opposite leg
5	1	moving sideways twisting trunk (trunk does the work, not the legs)	run forward	moving sideways, twisting trunk, facing opposite direction from first ladder
6	1	same as #1		
7	2	same as #2		
8	2	same as #5		
9	2	shuffle through ladder, alternating left, then right foot out of ladder	run forward	shuffle through ladder, alternating left, then right foot out of ladder
10	4	hopping sideways on one leg	run forward	hopping sideways on the opposite leg
11	1	same as #1		
12	2	same as #4		
13	2	hopping forward, both legs in rung, then legs on either sides of the rung	slalom	hopping forward, both legs in rung, then legs on either sides of the rung
14	1	same as #9		
15	4	run forward	run forward, touching both feet down between each hurdle	run forward
16	2	hopping forward with both legs	hopping sideways on both legs	hopping forward with both legs
17	2	same as #5	slalom	same as #5
18	2	run sideways, both feet go in each rung, one at a time	run forward	run sideways facing the opposite direction from the first ladder, both feet go in each rung, one at a time
19	2	same as #1		

Cool Down (10 minutes): Light jogging and stretching

After their showers, the players went up to the restaurant in the stadium for a healthy dinner (soup and sandwiches) and then did their homework under the supervision of the tutors hired by the club.

SAMPLES OF COORDINATION EXERCISES
FROM GLASGOW CELTIC

The teams shared much of the same equipment for their coordination training. The exercises below give a flavor for the work that each team did. While the drills clearly provided the players with a strenuous workout and a chance to improve their movement skills, they were held on the concrete floor of the concourse under the stadium. Especially for the pliometrics, it is a hard surface on which exercise.

Ladder with Gauntlet

Half of the players were "resting" as servers while the other half went through the course. The players would first move through a 20-rung agility ladder (using various techniques, similar to those in Table D1). They would then work their way down the gauntlet. Each server would have a ball. They would serve the player who was working and he would return the ball in various ways (e.g., pass, header, volley). The starting line and the locations of the servers were marked with cones.

Pliometric Boxes

Pliometric exercise is a form of training an athlete's explosive power by means of jumping exercises. For these exercises, many of the teams used wooden boxes approximately 20 centimeters in height. There were a

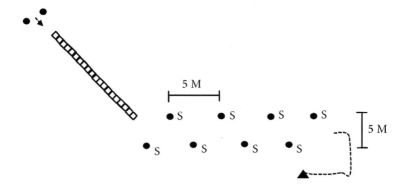

Figure D2. Under 13 Ladder & Gauntlet

number of pliometric exercises that the players undertook. For example, the players hopped onto and off of the box. They would also jump up and then jump down straddling the box.

Hex Drill

The hexagons were painted on the floor of the concourse under the stadium. The player would start at the center spot and hop out to each line and back to the center. The exercises were performed for a set time. The hexagon was one meter across. They could be done on one leg or both legs.

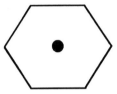

Figure D3. Hex Drill

Dot Drill

The dots were also painted on the floor of the concourse in the stadium. The players would complete various patterns during a set time. The patterns were done on one or both feet.

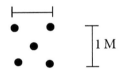

Figure D4. Dot Drill

Reaction Drill

The drill started with two players facing a coach with three red mini-hurdles on one side of each of them and three yellow mini-hurdles on the other side of each (see Figure D5). The coach held his hands behind his back; a small red ball in one hand and a small yellow ball in the other. He would hold up a ball and the player would have to sidestep over the three hurdles of the corresponding color. The coach could switch the balls from one hand to the other when they were behind his back. When he held out

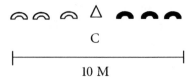

C

|———————————————|
10 M

Figure D5. Reaction Drill

the ball, the player had to look for the color, not which hand was holding the ball. The exercise was also a race between the two players so that they would be forced to react quickly and move quickly.

COMBINATIONS OF COORDINATION TRAINING WITH TECHNICAL TRAINING

In the next two diagrams (pages 163 and 164), one can see ways to combine technical training with coordination training. By comparing the two exercises from FC Barcelona, one can see how they are similar, but age appropriate. The exercise for the older players is much more complicated.

Football School (six- to seven-year-olds) Shooting Exercise

The shooter must first run a certain pattern over the four poles laid out on the ground (see Figure D6). He then runs forward to shoot the ball with his first touch. After shooting, he goes to get the ball and returns it to the server. The players rotated being the server and the goalkeeper. The patterns over the poles were:

1. Sidestep through
2. Sidestep through, back, and through again
3. Hop over with both legs sideways

There were two stations for this exercise side-by-side so that the players could shoot with both feet and go over the poles to their left and right. They alternated lines.

Coaching Points: Although the coach only commented on the results of the players' attempts, one can point out aspects of proper shooting technique. If one is focusing on the agility training aspect of this exercise, the coach's comments should focus on the player's navigation of the poles.

Cadet (15–16-year-olds) Team Shooting Exercise

The exercise alternated sides. There was no goalkeeper. The wing and

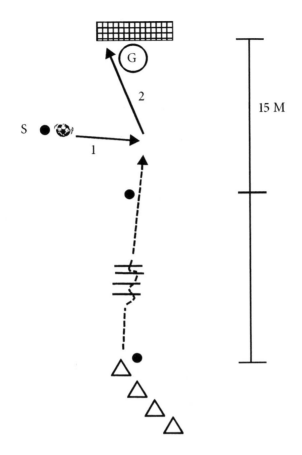

Figure D6. Football School Shooting Exercise

the shooter would start at the same time. The coach adjusted the shooter's tasks until the timing was right for him to have to run for the cross. The players rotated across the field to the four starting positions. The servers were changed periodically.

Winger: Dribble through the flags and pass to the server. After passing, run through the poles, run around the cones, jump the hurdle, do a somersault, receive the return pass and cross it for the forward.

Forward: Jump one hurdle, then the next, run through the flags, run tight circles around the last two flags, run through the poles on the ground and around the last cone to finish the cross.

Variation: Only the middle two tracks were used. Two players would race, each through his own track (although the tracks shared two

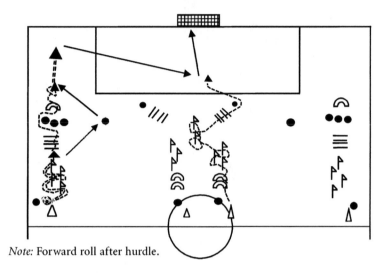

Note: Forward roll after hurdle.

Figure D7. Cadet Finishing Coordination Exercise

obstacles) and as they neared the top of the penalty area, a coach would drop a ball for them to race for and score.

As one can see in the two examples above, it is possible to combine coordination training with technical training. Another example from Slavia Prague: The Under 10 team was divided into four groups. There were five stations at which they spend approximately seven minutes each. At each station, they completed a number of repetitions through a dribbling/coordination course. For example, at one station, the players would pass their ball under a small hurdle, then run around the hurdle and collect the ball on the other side. At another station, the players dribbled up to a flag, then turned away to the next flag. The flags were arranged in a zig-zag pattern. There are many possibilities for such courses, limited only by a coach's imagination.

Appendix E

Technical Training

As I wrote in Chapter 4, there were no special new ways to train technique (or tactics). The key was a lot of repetitions to increase the speed and consistency of a skill.

Some technical exercises and game exercises are below. At FC Barcelona, technical training was often combined with coordination training (pages 162–164) or pattern play (described below). The key for them was to find a way to put the players under increasing pressure so that their ability to carry out a technique would remain strong in spite of fatigue or pressure.

I saw little of the "Coerver Moves" method of training, other than as a warm-up. The "Coerver Method" is a way of learning 1 against 1 moves by repetition, moving across the field without any pressure from opponents or boundaries. There are important agility elements in doing the moves. The problem with the method is that there are no defenders, teammates, or space restrictions. Therefore, players don't really learn how or when to use the moves in games. The clubs I visited preferred to have some element of decision-making in their technical training

As a reminder of the symbols in the diagrams, the Key is repeated on next page.

Combined Passing and Dribbling Activities

Glasgow Celtic's Under 13 coach, Martin Miller, had names for many of his training exercises so that his players would be able to remember how to execute them. Below are two exercises for technical training from his repertoire.

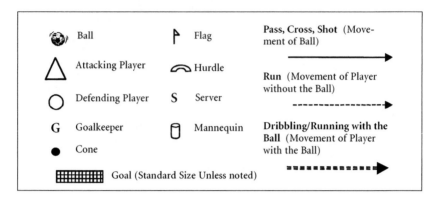

"Motherwell Routine"

Coaching Points: The passing part of the exercise should be done with one touch by each player. The servers must be active, receiving the ball with their bodies sideways.

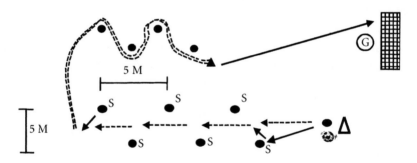

Figure E1. "Motherwell Routine"— The player advances down the gauntlet playing wall passes with the servers. After receiving the last pass, he dribbles through the cones, and shoots at goal. Note: To keep the diagram clear, not all passes are shown.

"Blackburn Routine"

There were a number of variations of the exercise. The first variation worked as illustrated in Figure E2. Other variations included two players completing a takeover: one or even two wall passes before one of them would pass the ball on to the next player. For example, 1 would pass to 2 and move into a support position. 2 would pass back to 1, who would pass back to 2. 2 would then pass to 3 and the game would continue in similar

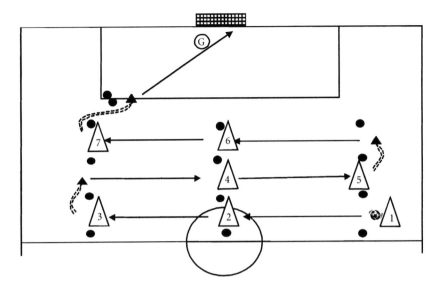

Figure E2. "Blackburn Routine"—Exercise should be done from both sides. Players follow their pass and replace the player to whom they pass (1 to 2, 2 to 3, and so on). The last player (#7) uses a fake to go by the last two cones and then shoots on goal. He then goes to the starting line. There are a number of variations (see explanation above).

fashion. In every variation, the coach constantly encouraged players so that their activity was sharp.

Coaching Points: When a player in the center receives the ball, his back should be to goal and he should receive it with his back foot in order to protect the ball. When a player on the outside receives the ball, he should receive in facing forward, but also with his back foot. A player receiving the ball should remember PARS. PARS is an acronym for Point (where you want the ball), Angled Run (to make space and position your body correctly), and Shout (to tell your teammate to pass). After passing the ball, the passer must work to "lose" his imaginary defender. The coach's guidelines were the three A's: Away (from the defender), Across (or Angle, in other words make it difficult for the defender to see both you and the ball), and Accelerate (sprint to get away from the defender).

Forward Runs, the Final Pass, and Finishing

There were three variations for this shooting exercise from Newcastle United. The organization for each was similar. The server played the ball to the wide player, alternating sides, who, in turn, played the ball to the forward for him to finish. After a turn in the wide position, the player would take a turn as the forward, and then go to the other side (see Figures E3, E4 and E5). In each the key was pass #2. The quality of the "entry" pass determined the quality of the chance to score.

First Variation (see Figure E3): The wide player takes one touch and then plays pass #2 with the inside of his left foot or the outside of his right foot (opposites on left side). The center forward makes the diagonal run and shoots first time. If the pass draws him too wide he should cross. The wide player makes a bending run into the center of the area to look for a rebound or to finish a cross if necessary.

Coaching Points: Wide player must make a good first touch to get the ball out from under himself, his second touch should be a carefully weighted pass which leads the forward into a shooting position. He should also disguise the pass by looking away. The forward should play first time, either a shot or a cross.

Second Variation (see Figure E4): Forward checks away then comes toward the wide player. When he receives pass #2, he uses his back foot to make a preparation touch and then shoots. The wide player must play pass #2 hard.

Coaching Points: The forward's control must be right to control the hard pass in a way that his second touch is a shot on goal. The coaches added the condition that the wide player had to do 20 push-ups if he neglected to follow for a rebound.

Third Variation (see Figure E5): The forward makes the opposite movement from the second variation to free himself. He moves toward the wide player and then pulls away. The wide player chips the ball to him just beyond

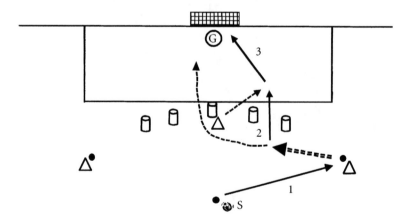

Figure E3. Forward Runs and the Final Pass

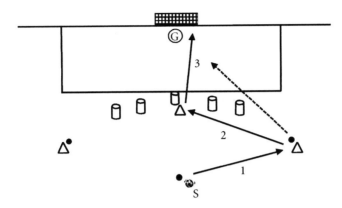

Figure E4. Pass to Center Forward for Shot, Follow for Rebound

the center mannequin. The forward has two touches, one to control and one to shoot the ball.

Coaching Points: Same as Second Variation.

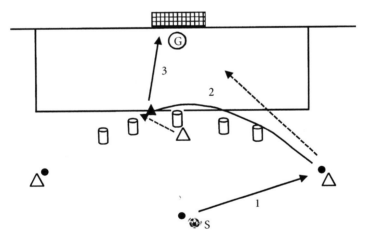

Figure E5. Chip to Center Forward for Shot, Follow for Rebound

"Pinball" Shooting Exercises with Mannequins in Front of the Goal

The shooting exercises below come from Newcastle United. All variations use the mannequins in front of goal. As the mannequins could not

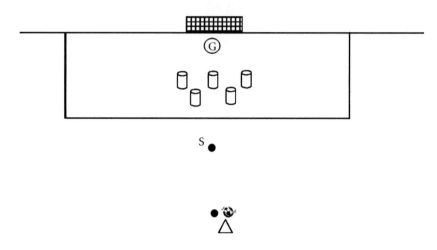

Figure E6. Shooting Exercises with Mannequins in front of the Goal

be firmly rooted, balls that hit them would usually land at their feet, creating a lot of goal mouth scrambles. It was like a pinball hitting the bumpers.

First Variation: Shooter passes to server who lays the ball off for a shot. Shooter must chase rebound (see Figure E6).

Coaching Points: Can the shooter use the mannequins to his advantage? There are also a lot of opportunities to test reactions in the penalty area.

Second Variation: The shooter and the server switch places and move to a wide position (where the penalty arc meets the top of the penalty area). The Shooter passes to the server, who plays the ball past and wide of the shooter. The shooter runs onto the ball and shoots with his first touch.

Third Variation: Attacker and defender play one-touch passes (parallel to goal line) to each other in the penalty arc. The attacker can turn and shoot when he wants. Both players follow up and try to score from rebounds (from the keeper or the mannequins).

Fourth Variation: Two players play one-touch passes (perpendicular to goal line). On the coach's signal, the one with the ball attacks the goal, both players look for rebounds. Either player can be on offense.

1 v 1 Duels

There are tactical and psychological considerations in 1 against 1 situations: When does one take a man on or when to tackle and which player has the more aggressive mentality? To win 1 v 1 duels consistently, a player must have excellent technique. Below are a few exercises for training 1 on 1 situations. The first two exercises are from Glasgow Celtic.

1 v 1, THEN 1 v 1 AGAIN

The attacker takes on each defender in turn and then tries to score. After his attempt on goal, he collects the ball and joins the line to go the other direction. The first defender is only allowed to play within the ten-meter-square grid. The second defender is only allowed to play along the line between the cones, but the attacker must go through the cones, not around them (see Figure E7).

Coaching Points: The attacker must be aggressive and try different fakes to go past the defenders.

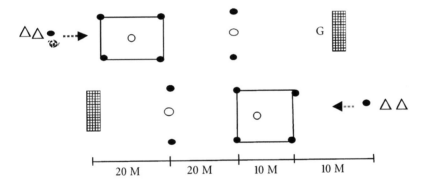

Figure E7. 1 v 1 Duel

DRIBBLING WITH SHADOW DEFENDER

This exercise comes from Newcastle United. As detailed in Chapter 5, the coaching at Newcastle was outstanding. The coaches used little phrases repeatedly, as a way to help the players remember the keys to successfully execute a technique.

For this exercise, there was a shadow defender, increasing the reality of the exercise (see Figure E8). At first, there was no ball, the defender was only shadowing the attacker. Next, the attacker's job was to dribble past one of the cones. He had to move his body and the ball in his attempt to race the defender past the cone. There was no tackling by the defender. Each player stayed on his own side of the line. The defender's task was to shadow the player with the ball and try to run past the cone toward which the attacker dribbled before the attacker arrived there.

Coaching Points: After playing with the ball for a minute, the coach encouraged the players to make one or two fakes and go for a cone.

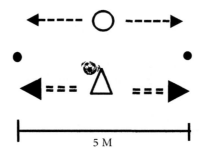

Figure E8. Dribbling with Shadow Defender

"MVV 2"

After a bout, the server goes to the attacking line, the attacker becomes the defender and the defender retrieves the ball and joins the servers' line (see Figure E9).

Coaching Points: The attacker must attack as quickly as possible to take advantage of the defender having to check to the second cone.

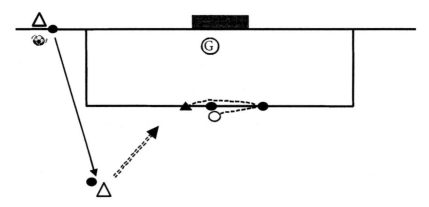

Figure E9. "MVV 2"—1 v 1 Finishing Exercise. When the coach gives the signal, the server passes the ball to the attacker and the defender must touch the other cone and then try to stop the attacker.

1 V 1 TO TWO GOALS

This game was played 1 v 1 in a grid ten meters square (See Figure E10). The defender played the ball to the attacker and then closed him down. The attacker had to attempt to score by dribbling through either of the goals (marked with flags). There were two grids to ensure that the players had a lot of repetitions. After a turn, the players would join the opposite line. The final five minutes of this exercise were a competition. All of the players were in one grid and they could stay in the attacking line as long as they scored. Once they failed to score, they stayed in the defending line. The game continued until there was only one player left in the attacking line.

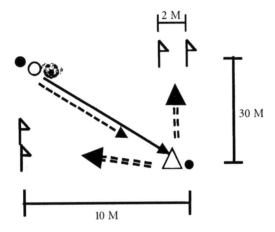

Figure E10. 1 v 1 to Two Goals

Coaching Points: The coach wanted the attackers to receive the ball sideways on with their back feet. Phrases of the coach were: "Control the ball, then attack" and "Keep the ball moving; if you keep the ball rolling, that is when you will go past players."

This exercise and the next came from Newcastle.

1 V 1 TO FULL SIZE GOAL

The exercise began when a server would play the ball to the attacker who would attempt to score (see Figure E11). The defender was allowed to be active once the server played the ball. The servers alternated. The other players switched between the starting positions so that they had the opportunity to attack and defend from both sides.

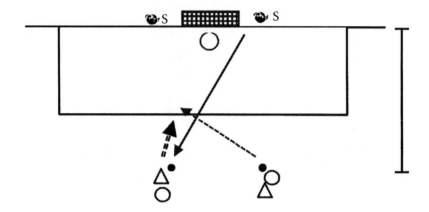

Figure E11. 1 v 1 to Full Size Goal

Coaching Points: For the attacker, phrases included: "Good first touch," "Receive with your back foot," "Keep the ball moving." For the defender, the key phrase was, "Make a yard." The coach meant that he wanted the defender to close down the attacker one yard at a time and not charge toward him.

Appendix F

Tactical Training

Tactical training is the teaching of decision-making. The aim of the following exercises is to help players make good decisions in a game. Coaches must decide how much control they want over defining a good decision. At Barcelona, all of the teams play with one of two systems and there is one set of decisions that is "correct." At other clubs, such as Newcastle United, good decisions were defined more broadly. More than one solution to a situation was acceptable. At Munich 1860, there was a hierarchy of decisions. Their belief is that it is best to play short passes as they are more likely to be accurate and controllable. If there is too much congestion, a long pass is fine, but as long passes are difficult to play accurately and to receive cleanly, they should not be the first priority.

The Key to symbols is included here as a reminder of the symbols in the various figures.

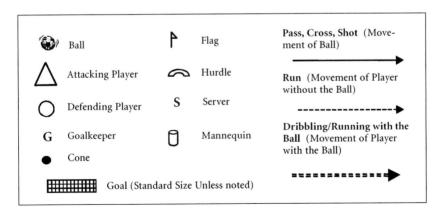

Key to Symbols in Diagrams

175

Team Shaping

At Glasgow Celtic, the coaches use the phrase "team shaping" to describe the way they prepare their teams tactically for their games. Below is the bulk of a training session of Celtic's Under 18 team. It includes three examples of attacking patterns, the "½ court" scrimmage, and set play practice. All of these activities are important elements of shaping the team, or preparing it tactically, for a game. The team worked on each for approximately five minutes. There were a few players at each starting point so that the play was continuous. Players stayed at one starting point throughout, thereby making the training functional. The exercises alternated between the right and left sides of the field, but only one side is shown for clarity.

First pattern (Figure F1): Player 1 passes to player 2 and then overlaps him into the corner. Player 2 dribbles inside and then passes to the corner for player 1 to cross. After passing, Player 2 should continue to the center to look for an opportunity to finish the cross. Play alternates from side to side. Only one side is shown in the diagram.

Coaching points: The winger (#2) must check away and then to the midfielder (#1) to create space for himself. As in all of these exercises, the forwards must time their runs so that they arrive at top speed. They must not be standing and waiting for the ball or they are too easy to mark.

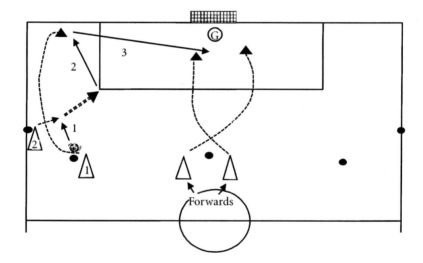

Figure F1. First Pattern of Finishing Exercise

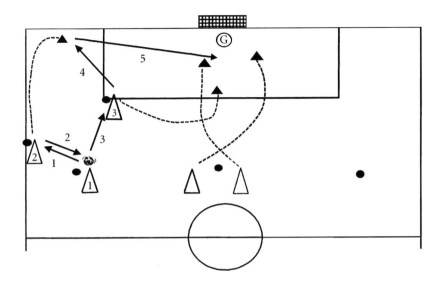

Figure F2. Second Pattern of Finishing Exercise

Second pattern (Figure F2): Players 1 and 2 complete a wall pass. Then player 1 passes to player 3. Player 3 passes to player 2, who has run down the line after playing to wall pass with player 1. Player 2 crosses the ball. After passing, player 3 should run into the center to prepare for the cross.

Coaching points: In addition to those in the first pattern, the target player (#3) must first turn inside when he receives the ball and then curl his run into the center so that his defender will not be able to see both the ball and him at the same time. When he receives the ball, he should receive it "sideways on" so that he can see forward and back at the same time.

Third pattern (Figure F3): A variation on the second pattern. Player 1 passes to player 2 and then moves into a supporting position behind player 3. Player 2 passes to Player 3 and then starts running down the line. Player 3 lays the ball off to player 1 and runs into the middle to be ready for the cross. Player 1 passes to player 2 in the corner so he can cross the ball.

Coaching Points: Same as first and second patterns. As this pattern is more complex, the timing of the runs must be more precise.

Scrimmage (32 minutes) The team played 8 v 7 + Goalkeeper on half of the field. The 8 attacked the regular goal while the 7 attacked two small goals on the halfway line. Regular rules were in effect.

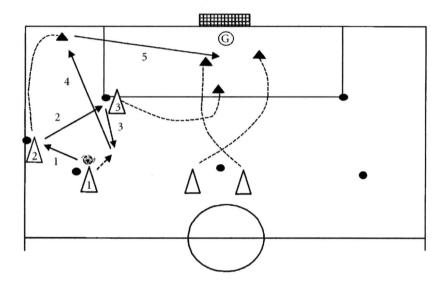

Figure F3. Third Pattern of Finishing Exercise.

The coach looked for the players to complete patterns from the previous segment of the training session. He also stopped play a number of times to point out ideas to various players. He wanted the defenders to force play toward the center of the field. To do this the marking backs were to "play the outside foot of the attacker." The coach also worked with the forwards on their spacing and the timing of their runs. In particular he wanted them to wait to make a run until the other forward had cleared out of the space into which they were going. Finally, they worked on a set play for throw-ins deep in the opponent's half (see Figure F4). The play

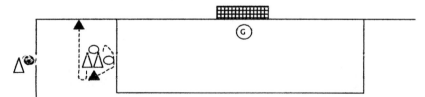

Note: Similar to an in-bounds play in basketball. One player moves to the endline and the other away from it. The first option is to throw the ball to the man on the endline, who can set the ball back to either of the other players. Other variations are possible.

Figure F4. Throw-In Play

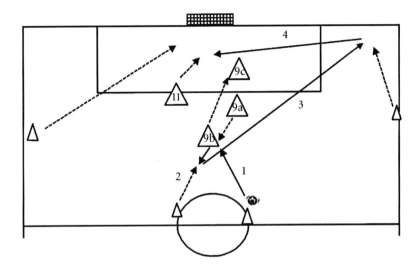

Figure F5. Liverpool Team-Shaping Exercise (one possible variation shown).

was much like an in-bounds play in basketball. The two players on the field try to screen the other player's defender as they make their runs, giving their teammate an extra second to play the ball.

Another idea for "team shaping" that Mr. McStay uses is an exercise he learned from the Liverpool coaches. In Figure F5, the shape is based on the front 6 players in a 4-4-2 system. There are two defensive midfielders, two wide midfielders, and two forwards. In the pattern shown, one center midfielder plays to a forward who lays the ball off to the center midfielder. The midfielder with the ball then plays the ball out to the wing. The wide midfielder crosses the ball for the other players, who have made runs into the penalty area. The idea could be adapted to any other system. The players can carry out any number of pre-planned or spontaneous attacking patterns.

Counterattacking Exercise (from Newcastle United)

This exercise took several minutes for the players to understand, but once they did, they not only had a lot of repetitions for counterattacking but also a good physical workout. During the early part of the exercise, one coach focused on the coaching while the other helped the players understand how to run the exercise. To keep the exercise moving, there were extra balls in each goal and teams waiting to counterattack behind each goal

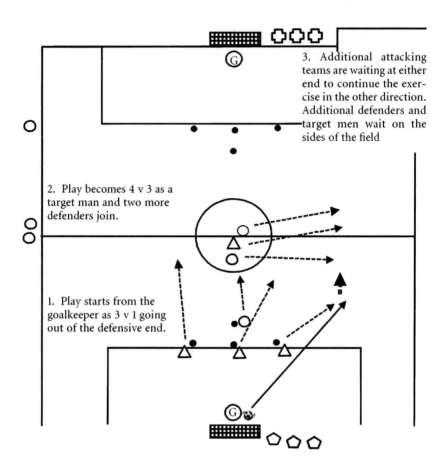

Figure F6. Counterattacking

(see Figure F6). The goalkeeper would start an attack by throwing the ball out to a defender. The attack would be 3 v 1 until around the midfield area where it would become 4 v 3. Once the attack finished, the team waiting behind the goal would step in to attack the other way and the attacking team would wait behind the goal they had just attacked for their next turn. Their forward and two more defenders would step on at midfield. When an attack broke down the responsible player would trade with one of the defenders. In this way the players rotated onto the defending team. The coaches were very active both in openly giving comment and praise and in talking with players one at a time while they were resting.

Coaching Points: The coaches wanted the attackers to attack quickly to press their advantage. They encouraged the players to make runs behind the defenders rather than wait for a safe square or back pass (offside was called). Some key phrases were: "Play forward," "Be clever with your runs," and "Great decisions." A number of the coaches' comments were on the subject of the decisions the players made. For the defenders, the main point was for the two at midfield. The coaches wanted one defender in front of the attacker and one behind him. The one in front could prevent the direct pass from the goalkeeper to the forward and attack the defender who received the ball.

"Keep Away"

Playing "keep away" is a popular activity in youth soccer training in the United States. The warm-up game 5 v 2 was also popular throughout the clubs I visited. Larger "keep away" games were not as popular as they are in the States, especially for older players. Most activities were more functional. The most interesting "keep away" game that I saw in the European clubs was at Munich 1860. It was interesting because they played first with a lopsided soccer ball and then with an American football. The different balls added an element of unpredictability that forced the players to react quickly and to be more agile in their movements.

Shadow Play

One of the instructors in the UEFA "A" license coaches' course, Jiri Nevrly, demonstrated a number of attacking patterns through *shadow play* (see Figure F7). While 11 v 0 or 11 v 1 (if there was a goalkeeper) is not realistic to the game, the shadow play did help the players with the timing of their runs and their ability to understand certain principles such as switching the point of attack. Without defenders clogging up the picture, it was easier for the players to see the movements of their teammates. A variation of the pattern play was that the team should not be more than 25 meters apart, from the back to the front. The idea was for the team to move in synchronization. Another aspect of the shadow play training was that Mr. Nevrly brought a diagram of the pattern onto the field and called the players around to look at it before they began to practice the movement.

Coaching Points: Even though there are no defenders, players must play quickly, even with one touch. Players must also make runs to the ball, not stand and wait for it. When players receive the ball, their body position must be correct: sideways, or facing forward if possible. After pass

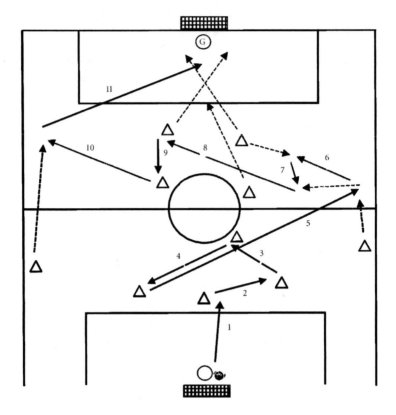

Figure F7. Example of Pattern Play

#10, several options are possible: a cross (as shown), an overlap by the midfielder, or a combination with one of the forwards.

Pattern Play at FC Barcelona

The Alevines B team (mostly ten-year-olds) concentrated during one training session almost totally on pattern play. I have outlined the entire training session below as a model.

1. First Exercise, with six variations (35 minutes: ten minutes for the first variation and five minutes for each of the others). In each variation, players follow to the next letter and E goes to A, which usually means they follow their passes, to prepare for their next repetition. The team used two grids so that there were only one or two players at each position, meaning

there was little margin for error. It also meant that the players had many repetitions in just five minutes.

First Variation (five minutes as shown and five minutes to the opposite side):

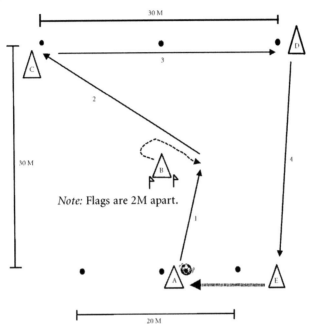

Figure F8. Exercise 1, Variation 1.

Coaching points: For all of the players, quality of passing is critical so that the following player can also pass with one touch. Player B must take two steps behind the flags (dummy defenders) and then check out and be sideways on so that he can play with his front foot to player C. The players were very disciplined about this.

Second Variation (five minutes): Players B and C complete a wall pass before C passes to D. (See Figure F9.)

Coaching points: Same as first variation.

Third Variation (five minutes): Player B plays the ball back to A, who plays it directly to C. B and C then complete a wall pass before C passes to D. (See Figure F10.)

Coaching points: In addition to those in the first variation, player C now signals player B by raising his arms over his head. One arm up means to do the second variation (B plays the ball to C for a wall pass). Two arms up means B should play the ball back to A to do the third variation.

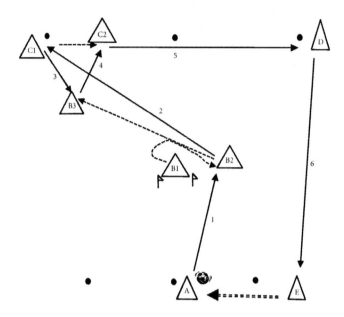

Figure F9. Exercise 1, Variation 2: Wall Pass between B and C is added.

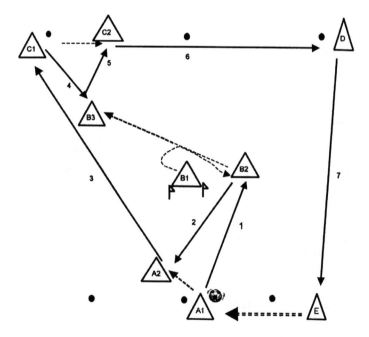

Figure F10. Exercise 1, Variation 3: Wall Pass added between A and B.

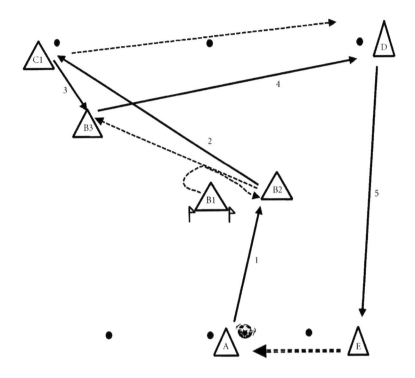

Figure F11. Exercise 1, Variation 4: After B receives the ball from C, he plays to D and C replaced D.

Fourth Variation (five minutes): B plays to C and receives a return pass. He then plays the ball to D. (See Figure F11.)

Coaching points: As above and Player C's signals are now one arm up for the fourth variation and two arms up for the third variation.

Fifth Variation (five minutes): Player B passes to C, receives a return pass, then plays a wall pass with player D. (See Figure F12.)

Coaching points: As above and Player B now completes two wall passes with the correct body angle and using his front foot to receive the ball. Player C's signal is now for player B to play the fifth variation (one arm up) or the third variation (two arms up).

Sixth Variation (no figure shown): The final variation brings together all of the previous exercises. B must check signals from C and D to determine which variation to do.

Coaching points: Player C signals for the third variation (two arms up) or the fourth variation (one arm up). Either way, as Player B receives the ball for the second time, he must now also check the signal from Player

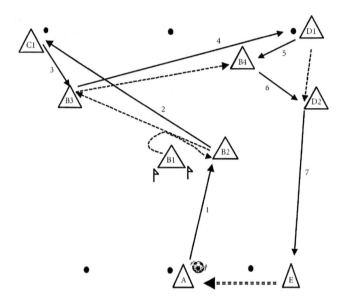

Figure F12. Exercise 1, Variation 5: Add Wall Pass between B and D.

D, one arm up to play back to Player C (third variation) and two arms up to play directly across to Player D (fifth variation). If the players can handle it, Players B and D can complete a wall pass before player D plays the ball to Player E.

One of the best parts of this exercise, in addition to the repetitions for technical mastery, is the element of decision making. Players must be aware of their teammate's signals so that they know where to pass the ball. It is a simple, yet realistic way to improve the players' awareness.

3. Second Exercise, with three variations (ten minutes each)

The second exercise added two components, longer passing and finishing on goal. Starting locations were given out by the numbers (see diagrams). Each group went in rapid succession, alternating sides (only one side is shown in the diagrams for the sake of clarity).

First Variation (10 minutes). (See Figure F13.) Player 9 works continuously (switching every two or three minutes), the other players rotate through the starting spots 4, 6, 4, 8, 4, 6 and so on. The coach used these numbers to organize the activity since they correspond to positions in their playing formation. The exercise alternated sides and again repetitions were following one right after the other. Player 9 was running from side to side, as if pulling away from his marker in a match. Pass 2 was a chip.

Coaching points: The distances indicated were for ten-year-olds on

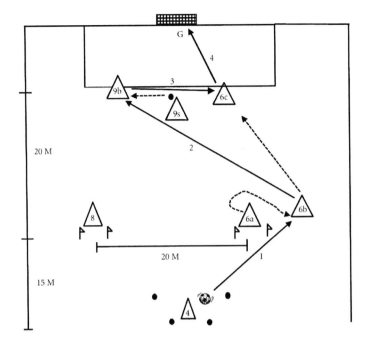

Figure F13. Exercise 2, Variation 1.

a field they were sharing with three other teams. Obviously, distances should be adjusted for age and ability of players (see similar exercise in Infantil A training below). As with the First Exercise, there is a great emphasis on technique and repetitions to refine it. Players 6 and 8 check in and then out and their body position is sideways.

Second Variation (ten minutes). (See Figure F14.) Play on one side at a time, five minutes each. Player rotate through the three positions. Pass 2 is a chip. Player who is shooting checks back to Player 4, then runs forward. The shooter has two touches, one to control and one to shoot.

Coaching Points: As above.

Third Variation (ten minutes). (See Figure F15.) Coaching Points: As above, the player who shoots also checks to 4 and then goes forward. The other midfielder (number 6 in diagram 9) checks in, then out, calling for the ball, but then lets it run past him to the winger (number 7 in the diagram) who has checked back. The winger must receive the ball sideways on with his front foot, carry the ball down and then cross.

Scrimmage (ten minutes) The final activity of training was a game 8 v 8 with one player who always played on the team with the ball (a "joker").

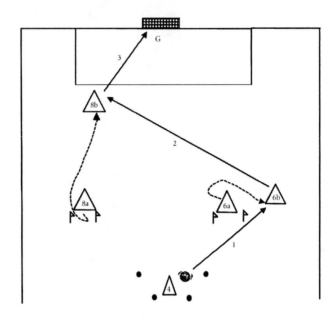

Figure F14. Exercise 2, Variation 2.

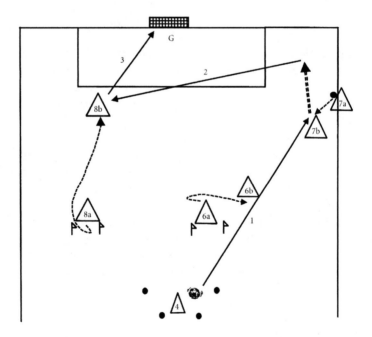

Figure F15. Exercise 2, Variation 3.

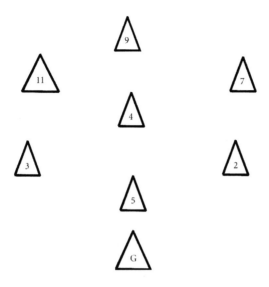

Figure F16. System of Play for Scrimmage.

There were full-sized goals and the field was 60 meters × 35 meters. The players were given positions which corresponded to positions in their match playing system (see Figure 16) and the "free" player was allowed to roam. He was indeed their "10" in their match on the Saturday. There was encouragement and comment by the coaches during the scrimmage, but no stopping to point out possibilities.

This training session was interesting for its simplicity of organization, for drills which had an element of decision-making, and for the clear way in which what occurred was geared toward the system of play the team uses.

Annotated Bibliography

Books

Bangsbo, Jens. *Fitness Training in Football: A Scientific Approach*. HO + Storm, Bagsvaerd, Denmark. 1994. Clear and detailed information on the types of fitness required in soccer and how to train them.

Barend, Frits, and Henk Van Dorp. *Ajax Barcelona Cruyff: The ABC of an Obstinate Maestro*. Bloomsbury, London. 1999. Transcripts of a series of interviews over the course of Cruyff's career as a player and coach.

Buzek, Mario, and Ludek Prochazka. *Ceská Fotbalova Školá [Czech Soccer School]*. Olympia, Prague. 1999. A guide to teaching soccer to children under the age of ten.

Cook, Malcolm. *Soccer Coaching and Team Management*. A&C Black, London. 1997. Basic ideas about organizing, managing, and coaching a team.

The FA Premier League Handbook (Season 1998-99). FA Premier League Ltd., London. 1998. The rules and regulations on every aspect of playing in the top level of English soccer.

Kormelink, Henny, and Tjeu Seeverens. *The Coaching Philosophies of Lous van Gaal and the Ajax Coaches*. Reedswain, Inc, Spring City, PA. 1997. A detailed account of every aspect of the soccer at Ajax Amsterdam from youth to professional teams.

Kormelink, Henny, and Tjeu Seeverens. *Developing Soccer Players the Dutch Way*. Reedswain, Inc, Spring City, PA. 1997. Many examples of the Dutch philosophy of player development.

Mosston, Muska, and Sara Ashworth. *The Spectrum of Teaching Styles: From Command to Discovery*. An older book, but with a useful way of breaking down the ways in which teachers work.

Psotta, Rudolf. *Fotbal Základní Program [School Football Program]*. NS Svoboda, Prague. 1999. A guide to coaching soccer for middle school physical education teachers.

Szymanski, Stefan, and Tim Kuypers. *Winners & Losers: The Business Strategy of Football*. Viking, London. 1999. Two economists analyze soccer as a business. The focus is on English teams.

Zitko, Miroslav. *Kompenzacni Cviceni* (Compensation Exercises). NS Svoboda,

Prague. 1998. Written by a gymnastics coach, includes exercises for players in other sports to develop their overall athletic ability.

Magazines

Fotbal a Trénink [Soccer and Training]. Noesis, Usti nad Labem, Czech Republic. The monthly journal of the Czech Soccer Coaches Association, primarily technical coaching articles and research of training methods.

FourFourTwo. Haymarket Specialist Publications, Ltd., Teddington, Middlesex, England. General interest soccer magazine that often has in-depth articles on training at various clubs. Focus is on English soccer.

Hattrick. Moraviapress, Breclav, Czech Republic. General interest Czech soccer magazine.

Insight. The Football Association, Potters Bar, Hertfordshire, England. FA Coaches Association Journal, primarily technical coaching articles and research of training methods.

Löwen News. TSV Munich 1860, Munich. Fan magazine of Munich 1860. The best soccer game program I have ever seen.

CD-ROM

FC Bayern Munich Junior Team. On Compact Disc. Description of the youth soccer training program at the club with many examples of training exercises.

Internet Web Pages (all accessed as of July 17, 2000)

Eastside Youth Soccer Association: *www.eysa.org*. EYSA Coaching Manual. Bellevue, Washington.

National Soccer Coaches Association of America: *www.nscaa.com*. The official web page of America's leading soccer coaches' association. Contains information on their many programs for coaches: symposia, convention, and courses.

Sporting Goods Manufacturing Association of America: *www.sportlink.com/ research/sport_specific/team/soccer_usa.html* Includes statistical information on the marketplace for soccer and other sports. A resource primarily for businesses.

EUROPEAN PROFESSIONAL CLUBS

AFC Ajax Amsterdam: www.ajax.nl
Arsenal FC: www.arsenal.co.uk
AJ Auxerre: www.aja.tm.fr
FC Barcelona: www.fcbarcelona.es

FC Bayern Munich: www.fcbayernmuenchen.de
Charlton Athletic FC: www.charlton-athletic.co.uk
Chelsea FC: www.chelsea.co.uk
Fulham FC: www.fulhamfc.ac.psiweb.com/football
Glasgow Celtic FC: www.celticfc.co.uk
TSV Munich 1860: www.tsv1860.de
Newcastle United FC: www.nufc.co.uk

Videos

Ajax Training Method Part 1: Coordination and Speed Training. Sport Video Productions. The Netherlands. The first in a two-part series about youth training at Ajax, focusing on how the players improve their physical abilities.

Ajax Training Method Part 2: Speed and Acceleration. Sport Video Productions. The Netherlands.

Safirikova, Jana. *Coaching Styles.* Made by a professor at Charles University in Prague, it uses team handball to show examples of the different teaching styles of Mosston and Ashworth.

Index